SHORT WALKS
—————PUBS IN—————
The Chilterns

Alan Charles

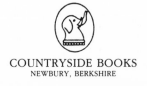

COUNTRYSIDE BOOKS
NEWBURY, BERKSHIRE

COUNTRYSIDE BOOKS
3 Catherine Road
Newbury, Berkshire

ISBN 1 85306 326 6

Designed by Mon Mohan
Cover illustration by Colin Doggett
Photographs and maps by the author

Produced through MRM Associates Ltd., Reading
Typeset by Paragon Typesetters, Queensferry, Clwyd
Printed by Woolnough Bookbinding Ltd., Irthlingborough

Contents

MAP SYMBOLS

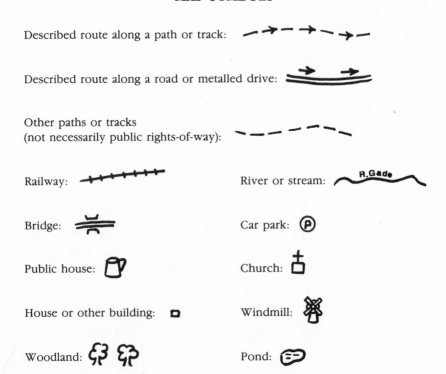

Described route along a path or track:

Described route along a road or metalled drive:

Other paths or tracks
(not necessarily public rights-of-way):

Railway: River or stream: R.Gade

Bridge: Car park: Ⓟ

Public house: Church:

House or other building: ▫   Windmill:

Woodland: Pond:

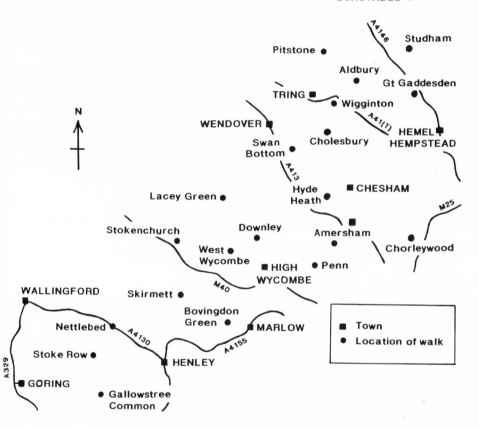

Area map showing locations of the walks.

Introduction

Few who have experienced the delights of the Chiltern countryside will be at all surprised that this piece of England has been labelled an Area of Outstanding Natural Beauty. Four counties share the mantle, Bedfordshire, Hertfordshire, Buckinghamshire and Oxfordshire, and all four are represented in this book — from Studham in the north (Bedfordshire) to Gallowstree Common in the south (Oxfordshire).

All of the walks are along public rights of way or permissive paths. They are chosen for their brevity (most are between 2 and 3 miles in length) and for their attractiveness and ease of navigation. Many include features which will interest young walkers — a children's farm, a river, an adventure playground, for example. For more mature walkers there will be added interest — in the fine houses and churches, restored windmills and historic landscapes, not to mention cricket on the village green!

Each walk is circular and based on a carefully chosen pub. Families are welcome inside all of these — not just in the garden. A minor variation on this occurs at the Pink and Lily, Lacey Green, where children under five can only be taken into the garden.

Pubs where food is highly priced have been avoided, as have those where there is, on Sundays, either no food or only a roast lunch, this being the most popular day for walking. While some of the pubs have a special children's menu, others offer children's portions at reduced prices. Self-sufficient families can eat their own food in a certain small number of the pubs, with the proviso that drinks are being purchased. Although I have mentioned which pubs these are, it would be good grace to check first with the licensee. Most of the pubs have their own car parks and are happy for customers to leave their cars there while on the walk. Again, please do remember to check first.

The Chilterns are featured on a variety of Ordnance Survey (OS) maps. These include the well-known Landranger series, on a scale of 1¼ inches to the mile, and the more recent Explorer series (nos 2 and 3), on a scale of 2½ inches to the mile. The latter are especially valuable to the walker since they show footpaths, field boundaries and other useful information in fine detail. The Explorer maps can be used for 17 of the walks; the remainder (Studham, Great Gaddesden and Chorleywood) can be followed on Landranger 166. Those familiar with grid reference numbers can use these maps to locate the exact position of each pub. The numbers are six-figures in length and appear after 'inn GR' in each chapter introduction.

Compass bearings are given throughout the text where these are thought to aid navigation. While stiles, gates, hedgerows and woodland are subject to the will of man, compass bearings are beyond his jurisdiction and remain (as far as makes no difference) just where they are.

Although I have fought shy of potentially difficult paths, I cannot entirely guarantee the absence of mud and nettles. As an antidote to these natural enemies three items of equipment and clothing are strongly recommended: trousers, good shoes (or wellingtons) and a walking-stick. With these on board there should be nothing between you and an enjoyable day out!

Alan Charles
Spring 1995

Publisher's Note

We hope that you obtain considerable enjoyment from this book; great care has been taken in its preparation. However, changes of landlord and actual closures are sadly not uncommon. Likewise, although at the time of publication all routes followed public rights of way or permitted paths, diversion orders can be made and permissions withdrawn.

We cannot of course be held responsible for such diversion orders and any resultant inaccuracies in the text which result from these or any other changes to the routes nor any damage which might result from walkers trespassing on private property. We are anxious that all details covering the walks and the pubs are kept up to date and would therefore welcome information from readers which would be relevant to future editions.

Pitstone
The Duke of Wellington

In a superb situation near the Grand Union Canal, the Duke of Wellington serves its time well — satisfying the needs of anglers, boat people, casual visitors and locals.

The regular menu includes door-step sandwiches, ploughman's lunches, 'Duke's Brunch' (a really good fry-up!) and omelettes. The home-made vegetarian dishes have appetising descriptions, typical examples being vegetables and cider hot pot with French bread or quorn and ale pie with fresh vegetables. Under the 'Home-made Meals' heading appear items such as chicken pie, pork in cider, and sweet and sour fish. The 'Two-course OAP Special' is very popular. Meals are served every day from 12 noon to 2 pm and 7 pm to 9.30 pm (9 pm on Sunday). A roast lunch is available on Sunday but the regular menu at that time has a slightly reduced choice. Children are welcome and can be accommodated in the dining area if eating.

The real ales are London Pride, Marston's Pedigree and Butcombe. The pub is open on Monday to Friday from 12 noon to 2.30 pm and 6 pm to 11 pm, on Saturday from 12 noon to 3 pm and 6 pm to 11 pm, and on Sunday from 12 noon to 3 pm and 7 pm to 10.30 pm. Dogs are not welcome inside the pub. Telephone: 01296 661402.

How to get there: The pub is close to the Grand Union Canal, ½ mile west of Pitstone village. You could take one of two roads signposted to 'Cheddington' from the B489 between Pitstone and Marsworth.

Parking: Since the pub's car park is used by the licensee's dogs when the pub is closed, you are asked not to leave your car there while on the walk. It is better to drive the first 200 yards of the walk (in the Cheddington direction) and leave your car in a parking area just beyond the canal bridge.

Length of the walk: 2 ¾ miles. Maps: OS Explorer 2 Chiltern Hills North or Landranger 165 Aylesbury and Leighton Buzzard area (inn GR 927160).

The first mile of this walk is southwards along the towpath of the Grand Union Canal, which is often busy with anglers and barging enthusiasts. The return route crosses peaceful countryside over the site of a 'lost' village and its manor house and a now silent wartime airfield. It concludes with a further ¼ mile of towpath and 'returns to base' by Pitstone Wharf. Lively with colourful barges, the wharf is noted for its canal cruises. It also has a gift shop and refreshment room.

The Walk

From the pub go left along the road (by car for safety) and cross the canal bridge to a parking area on the left. Join the canal towpath here (with the canal on your left) and stay with it for just under 1 mile to the next bridge — numbered 129. Notice the effect that years of towing has had on the metal guard protecting a corner of the bridge. Go under the bridge and cross a stile on the right immediately. Turn left on the farm track here and walk straight on between the barns of Manor Farm to a stile, then continue forward across a field to another stile. The 'circular walk' waymark on the stile marks the route of a 4-mile circuit from Marsworth, and we now follow these signs for the

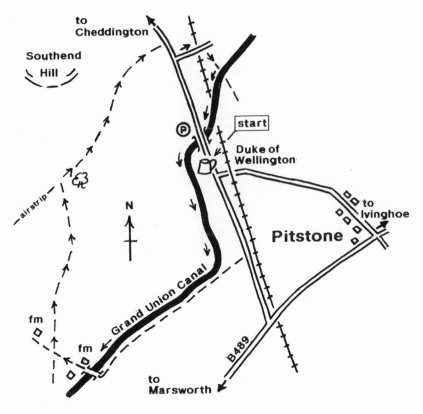

remainder of the walk. The numerous undulations in the fields hereabouts are vestiges of a 'lost' village and the De La Hay Manor House that once stood here.

Don't go forward to the next farm (Church Farm, now residential) but turn right immediately after the stile and walk the short field edge alongside a hedge to another stile. From that stile strike diagonally across the next field half-left to its furthest corner (10°) and then aim for the far end of the next, long narrow field. On arrival, a waymark will direct you briefly along the right-hand edge of a very large field to a footbridge over a ditch, from where you should go half-left across another field (350°). Southend Hill will be directly ahead as you cross that field towards the left side of a knot of trees. Before you reach those trees you will re-cross the ditch and a further part of the previous field.

Pitstone Wharf.

On arrival at a stile you may be aware that you have just crossed the extremity of a grassed-over airstrip. This was part of Cheddington Airfield during the Second World War.

From the stile, cross a tarmac hardstanding (doubtless part of the original airfield) to another stile near the opposite corner (60°), ignoring a farm track leaving that corner. Go over the stile and cross a field straight on towards, but not through, a metal farm gate (50°) on the left. Follow the left-hand edge of this very large field — with a ditch and hedge on the left — for ½ mile to a stile in its far corner, and join a road there.

Turn right at the road and soon go left into a 'no through road' and under a railway bridge. Go over a stone stile on the right immediately beyond the bridge and walk across a field, almost parallel to the railway embankment. Then cross another field and go straight on to a swing bridge on the canal. Turn right and follow the towpath (the canal is on the left) past Pitstone Wharf and under the road bridge to the car park. To return to the pub (or for refreshments at the wharf) cross this narrow bridge, but with great care if walking.

② Studham
The Bell

This attractive and unpretentious little village is home to one of the region's most comfortable and welcoming pubs — welcoming to adults and children alike. Where eating is concerned, the frequent use of the words 'home-made' is the guarantee of an enjoyable visit. The regular menu includes home-made pies and lasagne in addition to five varieties of locally produced sausages. Fish also comes in five varieties, and there is a good choice from filled jacket potatoes, ploughman's lunches and vegetarian dishes. Blackboard 'Specials' increase the choice further. Examples are Somerset pie (pork in cider and cream), Greek moussaka, and lemon chicken with rice. And the pleasure of eating at the Bell is extended by all the delights of the 'Sweet Naughties' board! Children can be taken into one of two 'no smoking' dining areas. If the day is good they will enjoy being in the garden, where there is a small slide, a swing and three white ducks. Meals are served every day from 12 noon to 2 pm and 7 pm to 9.30 pm (9 pm on Sunday). The same menu applies throughout, with the addition of a roast lunch on Sundays.

The real ales are Bass, Burton, Tetley and Flowers IPA, while lagers are Stella, Labatt's and Castlemaine. Drinking hours are from 11.30 am to 3 pm and 6 pm to 11 pm on Monday to Saturday, and from 12 noon to 3 pm and 7 pm to 10.30 pm on Sunday. Dogs may be taken into the garden or the Tavern Bar only.

Telephone: 01582 872460.

How to get there: Studham can be approached from the A4146 between Hemel Hempstead and Leighton Buzzard. Leave the A4146 at Hudnall Corner (near Fourways Car Centre) and follow road signs to Studham (2 miles).

Parking: In the pub's car park or near the memorial clock at the village crossing.

Length of the walk: 2 miles. Map: OS Landranger 166 Luton, Hertford and surrounding area (inn GR 023160).

This easy walk loops westward from Studham, crossing Studham Common and skirting cultivated fields. After a brief woodland episode and a close pass of the parish church, it returns to the Bell along a zig-zag field-edge route.

The Walk

On leaving the pub go left and down to the memorial clock at the crossroads. Turn right here into Church Road and, passing the Methodist church, leave the road opposite Swannells Wood (another road). Taking your direction from the bridleway finger on the signpost (not the footpath), walk just above the dip of the common, through the trees and slightly left of your previous direction (220°). You will soon be out in the open and heading towards a house, The Old School, at a road end.

Continue forward from the left side of the house and, ignoring a footpath going half-left, walk the right-hand edge of a sloping field. From the far end of this long field cross a road and follow the right-hand edge of another field. Initially taking guidance from overhead wires, aim for a stile and gate at the end of this field. Another set of wires will then lead you along the

13

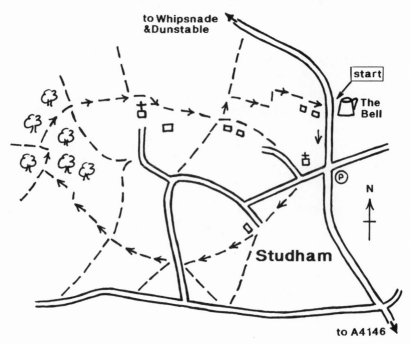

next field's right-hand edge. Ignore a stile or gap on the right quite soon and follow the wires into the field's far corner, near a cattle trough.

From a gate in that corner go forward 15 yards and climb a short flight of steps on the right. These will take you up to a path and under the trees of a splendid beech wood — Mason's Plantation. Continuing in the same direction as previously, you will in due course find yourself at the inner corner of this L-shaped wood by a metal signpost. Turn right at the T-junction here and walk deeper into the wood along a grassy track. Go left with the track after 80 yards (after passing a shed on the left) and turn right (20°) at a three-way signpost after a further 30 yards. When this very fine path through the wood meets a crossing, keep forward over a ditch (footbridge provided) to a stile and enter a meadow. Aim for the far left-hand corner of the meadow (80°), to the left of tall trees, and join a T-junction of cinder tracks. If you think you hear something that sounds very much like a steam engine, then you are right — it's the Great Whipsnade Railway at the Wild Animal Park!

The trees hide Studham's parish church. This is not the most attractive of churches from the outside, but a delight inside. Keeping forward so that the church and its trees are on your

14

Studham village.

right, walk the wide track until it soon turns right, then branch left across the grass to a metal signpost (120°), with Manor Farm in view on your right. From here follow a right-hand field edge to a four-way signpost in the field's far right-hand corner. Turn left and walk a left-hand field edge for 100 yards (leaving some of Studham's newer houses behind). Turn right at a signpost (110°), then walk another right-hand field edge and turn left from the field corner. The next and final signpost appears a couple of yards prior to the hedge corner. This directs you along a path under trees and back to the Bell.

Places of interest nearby

You could, perhaps, spend the remainder of the day just up the road at Whipsnade, where you will find the *Wild Animal Park* and the National Trust's *Tree Cathedral*.

3 Aldbury
The Valiant Trooper

Situated in one of Hertfordshire's most attractive villages, the Valiant Trooper traces its roots back at least 200 years. Originally the Trooper alehouse, the pub became Valiant in the late 1800s, and now expresses its age in the atmosphere and decor of its bars — in its low beams, tiled floors and open fireplaces. The regular menu offers sandwiches, jacket potatoes and ploughman's lunches. More substantial meals are listed on the blackboard and include (for example) mixed grill, steak and kidney pie, cottage pie and tortollini bolognese. Children are welcome in the Small Bar, a bar in name only, which is 'no smoking' at lunchtimes. Bar meals are served every day from 12.30 pm to 2 pm and 6.30 pm to 9 pm, with the exception of Sunday and Monday evenings.

The Valiant Trooper is noted for its good value real ale, which includes Abbot Ale, Bass, London Pride and (at a very attractive price) John Smith's. There is also a guest beer regularly on pump. Red and white wines are available by the glass, and an

Australian pink sparkling. Draught cider is Scrumpy Jack and lagers include Beck's, Coors, McEwan's and Tennent's. Drinking hours are 'all day' from Monday to Saturday (11 am to 11 pm), 12 noon to 3 pm and 7 pm to 10.30 pm on Sunday. Well-behaved dogs are welcome inside or in the very large garden, but should be kept on a lead.
Telephone: 01442 851203.

How to get there: The pub is in Trooper Road, Aldbury, north-east of Tring. If driving from Tring along Station Road, turn right into Trooper Road when you arrive at the village pond. Aldbury is one mile from Tring station, where there is a good rail service from London (Euston). Bus 27 runs from the station to Aldbury one-to-two hourly, Monday to Saturday.

Parking: In the pub's car park or near the village pond. Alternatively, you could leave your car in the public car park north of the village along the Ivinghoe road, ⅓ mile from the Valiant Trooper.

Length of the walk: 2½ miles. Maps: OS Explorer 2 Chiltern Hills North or Landranger 165 Aylesbury and Leighton Buzzard area (inn GR 964122).

Although there is a fairly steep climb at the start, this walk follows one of the easiest routes to the summit of the Ashridge estate. That's where the more energetic in your party can climb the 172 steps of the Bridgewater Monument (when open), while the others can, in the summer months, visit the National Trust shop and exhibition room or relax in the tea garden.

The monument, shop and information room are open from April until the end of October, every afternoon except on Fridays. The tea garden is open from Easter until mid-October, on weekend afternoons only. If you are walking this when everything is closed do not despair — it is a superb route and you will still enjoy the walk for the views on the way up and the woodland at the top.

The Walk

On leaving the Valiant Trooper turn left and left again into Newground Road. Soon go right with the road and left into Malting Lane, a 'no through road'. Follow this uphill to where

17

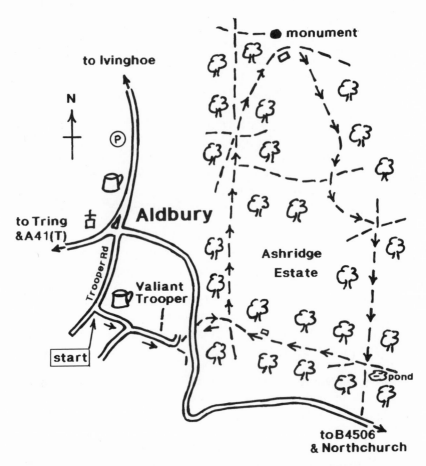

it becomes a private drive on the left, then go half-left on an uphill sunken path, signposted as a bridleway to Berkhamsted Common (50°). When this soon meets a road, cross to another sunken path and continue uphill under the trees. After crossing a path (also sunken), keep climbing and take the uphill right-hand branch after about 30 yards. This will place you on an open, grassy area. Now you should aim for the left-hand of the two seats situated along the upper border of this area. Passing under electricity wires here and crossing a ditch, go forward a further 30 yards to a wide track.

Turning left into the track (360° and under some very fine beech trees) you now have ½ mile of good walking all the way to the Bridgewater Monument. While you walk that ½ mile —

18

and enjoy the occasional view of Aldbury down on your left — you should ignore all lesser paths and tracks until you find yourself on a grassy area by the monument.

The monument was put up to commemorate the 3rd Duke of Bridgewater — the 'Father of Inland Navigation' and one-time owner of Ashridge — for his pioneering efforts during the early days of the canal age. In exchange for a moderate fee you can climb the monument, when it is open, and claim an excellent view of the Ashridge Estate and beyond, but you may prefer to spend the time and money in the nearby National Trust shop and tea garden!

To continue with the walk you should go half-right (160°) after passing the tea garden and a wooden shelter. This will take you under the trees and within 20 yards of a fenced meadow on the right. Keeping parallel to the fence and crossing a cinder track as you go, stay with the fence when it curves round to the right. When you find yourself close to the far left-hand corner of the meadow you should keep straight on over a waymarked crossing (blue arrow) and into a path that soon curves left (200° at the start). An informal 'no horses' notice will aid you in the navigation.

You will eventually arrive at a five-way junction of paths. Turn right here (180° — not acutely right) and make your way through the wood for almost ½ mile to a crossing-track, passing a short field edge as you proceed. There is a 'footpath only, no horses or cyclists' notice at the crossing and a large pond a short distance beyond it. Turn right at the crossing (290°) and keep to the main track as it meanders through the wood. Continue forward as you pass a cottage on the right (taking your cue from the blue waymark arrows) and soon find yourself on that open, grassy area met with near the start of the walk — complete with seats and overhead wires.

Keep straight on along the left edge of the grassy area (280°) and join a downhill path — following the first part of the walk but in reverse. A sunken path is crossed, and then a road, and another path takes you down to Malting Lane. Malting Lane meets Newground Road at a T-junction, where you should turn right for the Valiant Trooper. All that remains is to explore this delightful village and, if you feel so inclined, its other excellent pub, the Greyhound, or the tea room opposite.

4 Great Gaddesden
The Cock and Bottle

The Cock and Bottle enjoys a most attractive situation in the Gade valley, close to Great Gaddesden's flint-built village school, the parish church and Church Cottages. It held its first licence in 1806, when it was a cross between an alehouse and farmhouse.

The regular menu starts off with vegetarian meals — vegetable burger in a bun with chips and salad, cheese ploughman's, cheese and vegetable pizza, for example. Fish dishes include scampi, lemon sole and plaice. Next comes SLT's (a puzzle for the children!) beef burgers, jumbo sausages and chilli con carne. There are various non-vegetarian ploughman's and a choice of doorstep sandwiches. A roast lunch (beef or lamb) is offered on Sundays. Sweets include Danish apple pastry, hot chocolate fudge cake or treacle sponge pudding. Children's meals are sausages or fish fingers in company with chips and (of course!) baked beans. The licensee is happy for you to eat your own sandwiches in the garden when food is not available, provided you are buying drinks. To the real ale enthusiast the pub offers a varied experience, with handpump labels changed weekly from a vocabulary approaching 30 different brews. Lager drinkers have four labels at their disposal, cider drinkers two — Strongbow and Scrumpy Jack. With part of its dining area (no-smoking) out of sight of the bar, the pub is ideal for families. There is also a games room.

The pub is not open at all Monday to Thursday lunchtimes. It is however open for food and drink Friday to Sunday lunchtimes from 11.30 am (12 noon Sunday) until 3 pm. It is open for drinking Monday to Saturday evenings from 5.30 pm to 11 pm, Sundays 7 pm to 10.30 pm (food from 7 pm until 10.30 pm Friday and Saturday only). Bar meals are available at all of the food times. If you have no choice but to walk on Monday to Thursday you could take light refreshments along the walk at Longford Children's Farm, where a coffee shop is open every day from 9 am to 5 pm.

Telephone: 01442 255381.

How to get there: The pub is in Pipers Hill, a short distance from the A4146, 3 miles north of Hemel Hempstead.

Parking: In the pub's car park or in Church Meadow, a 'no through road' close to the pub.

Length of the walk: 2 miles. Map: OS Landranger 166 Luton, Hertford and surrounding area (inn GR 029112).

For views of the Gade valley this walk must be one of the best — but for any youngsters in your party the Longford Children's Farm might well take pride of place, along with the chance to paddle in the Gade!

The Walk
From the pub's car park go past the lovely old Church Cottages near the school and enter the churchyard. The church is worth a visit, if only to see the nave roof and the angels that hold it aloft. Passing to the left of the porch, look for a stile tucked away in the upper left-hand corner of the churchyard (not the gate lower down). When over the stile, turn right and follow overhead wires (parallel to the churchyard wall) as far as a dual

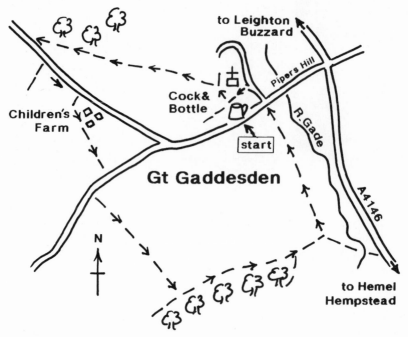

electricity pole with wires branching three ways. Go half-left here and uphill across the meadow to another pole in the furthest corner (290°), taking care how you tread the uneven surface. Pass through a hedge gap in the corner and continue in about the same direction, heading for the left-hand end of a wood. Cross a stile there and follow the left-hand edge of the wood to another stile in the sharp corner of a meadow. Turn left onto the road and, passing the Buddhist Centre, walk as far as a footpath sign at a dip in the road.

For Longford Children's Farm and its café continue forward 100 yards along the road.

Back in the dip, go through a metal gate by the corner of the farm and pass to the right of farm buildings — between the buildings and an adjacent garden fence. Soon turn left between fences and go over a stile into a field. Turn left from the stile and walk the field edge alongside the farm. Ignoring a gap onto the left, go all the way to a stile in the far left-hand corner of the field and join a road.

Longford Children's Farm.

Turn right on the road and left over a stile after 70 yards, then follow the left-hand edge of a very long field towards woodland at the far end. After entering the wood through a gap and passing to the left of a deep pit, go forward a few more yards to a T-junction in the path. Turn left here (70°) and walk under tall trees in this very fine wood. Ignoring all divisions in the path, and noting a field not far to your left, keep straight on through the wood until you emerge at a field corner.

Continuing forward between a hedge and a wire fence, you now have a superb view of the Gade valley, with the river Gade at Water End and Gaddesden Place directly ahead on the opposite hillside. The Place dates back to 1773.

From a pair of stiles at the bottom of the hill you could explore the river and a nearby pond by crossing a meadow on the right. There is a public footpath going in that direction. Otherwise, turn left and follow a field edge — with a hedge on your right — towards the houses at Great Gaddesden. Continue straight on from the far end of the field — over a stile and to the left of a pond — and soon find yourself back at the Cock and Bottle.

Wigginton
The Greyhound

5

The 'grand' appearance of the Greyhound contrasts markedly with the village in which it is set — a modest but attractive village close to the Chiltern escarpment. Enter the Greyhound and enjoy the comfort and the welcome, a welcome fully extended to all comers, including your canine companion. Children can be taken into one of the lounge bars, where, incidentally, two tables are reserved for non-smokers. If the weather is fine they will prefer the garden and its swings — that's if they haven't already spotted the marvellous adventure playground just down the road!

The regular food menu is impressive to say the least, with starters, fish, hot meals, salads, snacks and jacket potatoes. The hot meals range from the usual pub fare — from Cumberland sausage, lasagne, steak and kidney pie to chicken breast filled with Stilton sauce, and lamb cutlets with rosemary and red wine. Salads come in seven permutations, jacket potatoes in nine. Children's portions are available, as is a choice of desserts.

Senior citizens can enjoy a 25% reduction in the cost of a meal on any day. Meals are served from 11 am to 3 pm and 5.30 pm to 10.30 pm on Monday to Saturday, and 12 noon to 3 pm and 7 pm to 10.30 pm on Sunday, with a full menu at all of these times.

Where drink is concerned you are spoilt for choice, with five real ales at your disposal, two draught ciders (Stowford Press and Addlestones) and two draught lagers (Lowenbrau and Carlsberg). To say that the Greyhound specialises in wine is no exaggeration — there are 35 wines by the glass, 65 by the bottle! The pub is open for drinking from 11 am to 11 pm every day, except Sunday when times are restricted by law to 12 noon to 3 pm and 7 pm to 10.30 pm.

Telephone: 01442 824631.

How to get there: Wigginton is signposted from the A4251 and the A41(T), ½ mile east of Tring. On arrival at Wigginton drive along Chesham Road from the war memorial.

Parking: Park in the pub's own car park or in a parking area adjacent to the village adventure playground, a short distance south of the pub.

Length of the walk: 3 miles. Maps: OS Explorer 2 Chiltern Hills North or Landranger 165 Aylesbury and Leighton Buzzard area (inn GR 938100).

This is one of the easiest and most straightforward walks in the book. It follows ¾ mile of the 85 mile Ridgeway long distance trail and ½ mile of the enigmatic Grim's Dyke. Here the dyke runs as straight as a die through woodland, under a scattering of fine oak and beech trees and across cultivated fields.

The Walk

Turn left on leaving the Greyhound and left again into Wick Road. Stay with Wick Road to its end and continue forward on a wide, stony track. You will soon pass a signpost announcing the Ridgeway Path. This is a 'national trail' stretching from Ivinghoe Beacon (5 miles north of Wigginton) to Overton Hill in Wiltshire. As you now sample ¾ mile of the trail it would be

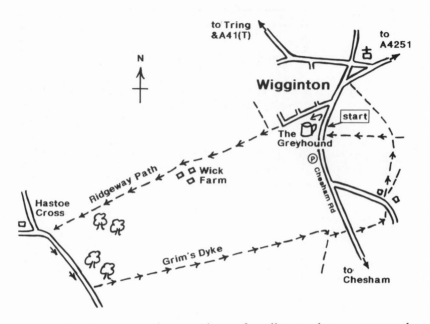

interesting to count the number of walkers who appear to be taking up the challenge of the full 85 miles — judged by the size of their backpacks, perhaps!

The track passes Wick Farm and continues straight on for a further ½ mile, meeting Kiln Road at Hastoe Cross. Turn left on this wide but fairly quiet road and stay with it for ¼ mile until you see a footpath signpost under trees on the right. Leave the road by turning left in the 'Wigginton 1' direction. This will take you over a stile and into a wood, where Grim's Dyke becomes immediately apparent. This linear dyke pops up in a number of places in the Chilterns and may have served as a civil boundary in Bronze Age times.

The path follows the dyke as it runs at right angles to the road, just inside the wood, with a corresponding ditch along the adjacent field edge. After leaving the wood it continues straight on under a scattering of oak trees. It crosses a farm track and continues forward, soon between open fields and eventually meeting a hedge head-on at the far end. (Did you notice at which point the dyke faded out completely?)

Turn right by that hedge and go with it for 30 yards to a stile

Wick Farm.

on the left, then resume your previous direction by crossing a field to a stile and road. For a speedy return to Wigginton and the pub you could go left along the road for just ⅓ mile (there is a grass verge or pavement for much of the way), but for a little more of God's good countryside (½ mile!) go right in the road for 20 yards and cross to a signposted path under trees. Follow the path as it passes between ponds, meanders through the scrub and runs between meadows, finally going left to meet a road opposite Osborne Cottage.

Turn left on the road and go down to its lowest point, adjacent to a pumping station. Turn right here into a short, wide track and walk uphill across the centre of a field. Pass to the right of a manhole cover and go through a gap in the far left-hand corner of the field. This will place you on a path between fields (340°), with a fence to the left and a view of Wigginton's church steeple directly ahead. Walk only as far as a signposted crossing at the lowest point of the path and climb a stile on the left just there. Cross the left-hand field along its dip to a hedge gap, then continue forward across a meadow to the road and the Greyhound.

6 Cholesbury
The Full Moon

This beautifully refurbished pub overlooks Cholesbury and Hawridge Commons, popular areas of grassland, trees and scrub criss-crossed with footpaths and bridleways. As two cottages, the pub is said to have existed before 1690, with parts dating back a century or more before that. It was once called the Half Moon and became 'Full' in 1820.

The varied and interesting bar menu starts with 'Appetisers' and moves on to 'Grills and Fries' — mixed grill, garlic chicken goujons, beef and Guinness sausages and gammon steak, for example. Vegetarian dishes include home-made vegetable pie and Cajun vegetable casserole on a bed of rice. Under the 'Meat and Fish' heading there is a selection of interesting dishes, ranging from the familiar steak and kidney pie cooked in ale to grilled Barbary duck in apple and ginger sauce. The menu concludes with rolls and sandwiches, ploughman's lunches and filled jacket potatoes. All this is available from 12 noon to 2.30 pm and 6.30 pm to 9.30 pm every day, with the exception of Sunday evening, and with the same menu applying throughout. Children are welcome here, the Stairs Bar being ideal for family meals.

The best sellers from the range of six real ales are from Morrells, Ruddles and Courage, and the three draught lagers are Carlsberg, Kronenbourg and Foster's. Old English cider and Beamish stout are also on draught. The drinking hours are 12 noon to 3 pm and 6 pm to 11 pm on Monday to Saturday, and 12 noon to 3 pm and 7 pm to 10.30 pm on Sunday. Dogs are allowed inside the pub and in the garden, but only if kept on a lead.

Telephone: 01494 758262.

How to get there: The pub is 4 miles north of Chesham on a comparatively quiet road. Approaching from Chesham via the A416 Berkhamsted road, follow road signs to 'Hawridge' and 'Cholesbury' when the A416 turns sharp right to go uphill.

Parking: In the pub's car park or alongside the common nearby.

Length of the walk: 2½ miles. Maps: OS Explorer 2 Chiltern Hills North or Landranger 165 Aylesbury and Leighton Buzzard area (inn GR 937069).

Few short walks can offer such a feast of pleasure and interest! You will see Cholesbury windmill and the impressive ditch and ramparts of Cholesbury Iron Age Camp, the lovely St Lawrence's church viewed across quiet meadows, as well as Cholesbury Common and its cricket green. All these are linked together by some fine Buckinghamshire countryside.

The Walk
From the Full Moon turn left, then left again into Rays Hill, which is signposted to 'Bellingdon'. After walking along this road for a short distance, you will have a good view of Cholesbury's windmill. The mill was built in 1884 (replacing an earlier one) and ended its working life in 1915. It is now a private house, and its sails are dummies! Walk to the bottom of the hill to where the road turns left, then go over a stile on the right and enter a meadow. Keep to the valley bottom across a

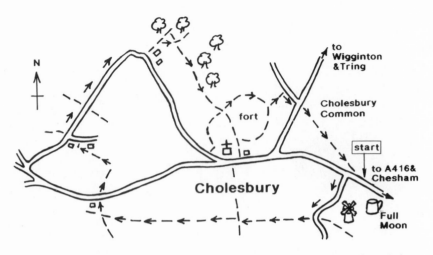

series of meadows and stiles until you arrive at an electricity
pole, then make your way forward to the far right-hand corner
of the next, the fourth, meadow.

From a stile in that corner continue forward yet again, but
now along the right-hand edge of two fields in succession, with
a hedge on the right and a line of Scots pines in view ahead. On
arrival at those pines, don't go forward over the stile in the field
corner but turn right and follow overhead power lines uphill to
the road adjacent to Chiltern Motors. Cross to the path opposite
(not the metal gate) and, ignoring a branch on the left, go
straight on through a double line of trees. This will lead you to
a stile and into a field. Turn left in the field immediately and go
through a gate in the corner, then aim for another gate at the
far left-hand corner of a paddock (300°). After a short track
takes you to another gate, turn right through the stableyard of
Broomstick Farm and join a road.

Turn left on the road and soon arrive at a quiet road junction
by Stone Cottage. Turn right here and follow the road in and
and out of a dip and up to Parrotts Farm at a corner. Go over
a stile to the left of the farm and cross a triangular meadow to
a stile under trees. Turn right just inside the wood and, keeping
within a few yards of the wood edge, advance about 75 yards
to a stile on the right. Having emerged into another meadow
keep to its right-hand edge, soon going back under trees from
a stile in the corner.

30

Church of St Lawrence.

With a field edge running parallel, a few yards to the right, go straight on through the wood (150°), ignoring (for once in your life!) the waymark arrows, which may cause some confusion. You may see a notice here announcing the 'Small Woodlands Project'. The Project is an offshoot of the Chiltern Society and offers expert advice to landowners on the planting and maintenance of small woodlands. The trees planted here are an example of this work.

The path comes out into the open yet again and, after passing under electricity wires, goes back under the trees. These tall trees line the impressive ditch and banks of Cholesbury Camp, a 15-acre Iron Age fort. Excavations in 1932 revealed pottery and hearths dating back to the 2nd century BC. Before turning left here, cross the ditch to a gap on the opposite side, and from there enjoy a view of St Lawrence's church, with its attractive wooden bell tower and its fine saddleback roof.

Back at the ditch — on the side that you came in — make that left turn, and walk the outer bank, with the ditch now down on your right. Ignore all turnings until you arrive at a wide crossing linking field to field (both gated), via the ditch. Back-step a few yards and leave the camp by turning left (relative to your previous direction) into a path. A hedge and one of those fields will then be on your right as you make your way to a road — through what can only be described as a wilderness area!

Turn right onto the road (Shire Lane) and go along this to a T-junction. Leave the road here by going straight on across Cholesbury Common. Branch half-right at the first junction of paths (160°) and follow a series of little white men (waymarks on wooden posts!) until you are out on the open area of common. The cricket green will come into view, also the windmill and the Full Moon pub.

As you approach the Full Moon, notice the boundary stone on the common nearby. From the inscription you will conclude that the pub is in Hawridge — but by only a few yards.

⑦ Swan Bottom
The Old Swan

A lovely 16th century pub, off the beaten track and surrounded by much fine countryside. The comfort and atmosphere here are no less than perfection. There are log fires on cold days, tiled floors and original oak beams (take care if you are more than 6 ft tall!).

Summarising the food choices is no easy task. With many of the raw materials arriving fresh from the market-place, the menus are likely to vary widely. They are likely to include pie or casserole of the day, mixed grill and honey roast ham. The pub is especially proud of its fish dishes, often using fresh halibut, turbot and Dover sole. Sandwiches, ploughman's lunches and jacket potatoes are available, and there is 'always something for kids!'. Most of the sweets are home-made — apricot crumble, pavlova, brandy cream crunch, for example. Meals are available from 12 noon to 2.15 pm and 7 pm to 9 pm daily, except on both Monday and Sunday evenings. Children are made welcome, and can use either the restaurant area

33

(where there is no smoking during meal times) or the very large garden.

There are four real ales — London Pride, Bass, Morland and the exceptional Butcombe from Bristol. The pub is open for drinking on Monday to Friday from 12 noon to 3 pm and 6 pm to 11 pm (with possible extensions in summer), 12 noon to 11 pm on Saturdays, and 12 noon to 3 pm and 7 pm to 10.30 pm on Sundays.

Telephone: 01494 837239.

How to get there: The pub can be approached from the A413, Aylesbury to Amersham road. Take the turning signposted to 'Kings Ash' and 'The Lee' (Rocky Lane near Cornwall Garages) 1½ miles south of Wendover, and drive along this road for 2 miles to Swan Bottom, turning left at the first crossing.

Parking: In the pub's large car park. You could, alternatively, park opposite the pub or near the crossing in Swan Bottom.

Length of the walk: 3 miles. Maps: OS Explorer 2 Chiltern Hills North or Landranger 165 Aylesbury and Leighton Buzzard area (inn GR 902055).

A most pleasant and uncomplicated walk, circling the valley known as Swan Bottom. It includes woodland and field edges and the main street at Lee Common, an attractive village of old and new houses.

The Walk
On leaving the Old Swan turn right and go left over a stile opposite Cygnet Cottage — behind Jim's Seat (Jim lives in Cygnet Cottage!). Following overhead wires, walk the wide, grassy swathe until it opens out to become a field. Cross one of two stiles at the far end of this field and turn right into a path under trees. Follow the path downhill to the road at Swan Bottom. Cross this and walk uphill on a rough drive, following overhead wires and passing to the left of paddocks. A series of stiles and left-hand field edges will take you straight on to a T-junction with a level path under trees. Turn left into this path and stay with it when it eventually enters replanted wood-land — ignoring a branch going half-right at that point.

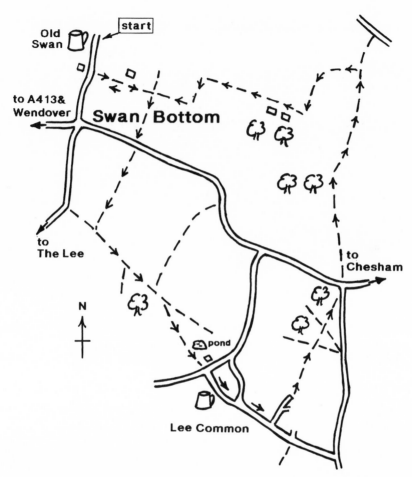

Turn half-right when you leave the wood and cross a field to the right-hand border of a clump of trees (150°). Reverting to your previous direction, and with the trees and a pond on your immediate left, follow the field edge to a stile and out to a road. Keep forward from the T-junction here (Oxford Street, no less) and walk through the lovely village of Lee Common. Having passed the Bugle pub and the Methodist church, turn left into Crockets Lane, which is just beyond Martins and marked with a footpath sign. Ignore a branch in the lane and keep straight on to its end by a house called Yellowstocks. Continue forward on a narrow meandering path under holly trees and out into a field.

Bugle Cottage, Lee Common.

Follow the short right-hand hedge and strike across the field in line with that same hedge (20°). From a stile at the far end of the field go straight on through a wood along a well-marked path (30°). Ignore all crossings and branches and keep forward until you reach a road to the left of a T-junction. Cross the road to a stile opposite and follow the right-hand edge of a field to its far corner. From here a path takes you into a dip and along a short wood edge (with the trees on the left). Climb the slope along a left-hand field edge and move to a right-hand edge when in the next dip, soon joining a farm track at a bend. Turn left onto the track and go with it as it curves round to the left. On reaching a pig farm at the top of the hill, turn right so that the buildings are on your left.

After walking the whole length of the buildings continue forward, firstly alongside a hedge and then between hedges. Go left with the hedges quite soon and then right into a narrow path after 130 yards. This will take you through a gate and along the short right-hand edge of a meadow to a crossing-path. Cross the stile here and continue forward until you are back at the road near the Old Swan.

8 **Lacey Green**
The Pink and Lily

The poet Rupert Brooke spent many happy hours at the Pink and Lily, finding refreshment of body and mind after his walks through the Chilterns. How much it has changed since his day I'm not sure, but I doubt that he could have been as spoilt for choice and quality in the food and drink as we are. The menu includes all the familiar pub meals, such as shepherd's pie, lasagne, chilli con carne, steak and kidney pie, chicken and so on. There are fish dishes and one or two specifically vegetarian dishes, although vegetarians would doubtless be happy with some of the nine permutations of filled jacket potatoes, or the ploughman's lunches. Sandwiches are many and various and come toasted, untoasted and jumbo-sized. A 'selection of home-made sweets' rounds off the standard menu and a specials board adds further variety. Meals are served between 12 noon to 2 pm every day, and, in the evenings, from 7 pm to 9 pm on Monday to Thursday and 6.30 pm to 9.30 pm on Friday and Saturday. The regular menu applies throughout.

There are no less than eight real ales, including Brakspear, Hobgoblin and the locally brewed Beechwood. The draught cider is Blackthorn Dry and lagers are Heineken, Foster's and Kronenbourg. There is a choice of six different wines by the glass. The pub is open for drinking from 11.45 am to 3 pm and 6 pm to 11 pm on Monday to Friday, 11 am to 3 pm and 6 pm to 11 pm on Saturday, and 12 noon to 3 pm and 7 pm to 10.30 pm on Sunday. Children are admitted into the Bottom Bar, but only if they are aged five or over. Parents of younger children must hope for good weather, so that they can take their charges into the garden. Well-mannered dogs may be taken inside.

Telephone: 01494 488308.

How to get there: The pub is in Pink Road, 1 mile north of Lacey Green. There are a number of possible routes from the A4010 in the Princes Risborough area. If approaching from the centre of Princes Risborough, join New Road near Budgen's store. Stay with this when it becomes Brimmers Road and turn left at a T-junction into Wardrobes Lane (signposted to 'Great Hampden'). The pub will be facing you at the end of Wardrobes Lane.

Parking: In the pub's car park or along Pink Road nearby.

Length of the walk: 3½ miles. Maps: OS Explorer 2 Chiltern Hills North or Landranger 165 Aylesbury and Leighton Buzzard area (inn GR 827019).

This walk enjoys the quietness of Lily Bottom Lane and a delightful coombe above Highwood Bottom, a haven of grass, hawthorn and birds. It ascends Kiln Lane (a gravel track) and aims for Lacey Green and its windmill, returning to Lily Bottom Lane across a series of level fields and a tiny bit of Grim's Dyke.

The Walk
From the Pink and Lily turn right into Lily Bottom Lane and, passing Hillock Cottages on the right, follow the quiet lane downhill for ⅓ mile to Lily Bank Farm. Stay on the lane as it continues forward and evolves into a track by The Barn and Lily

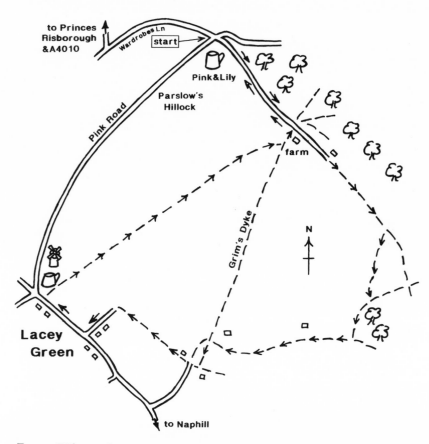

Farm. Where the track starts its main ascent look for a stile and signpost on the right and join a path running half-right from there. The path passes between a hedgerow (better described as a 'treerow') and a lovely coombe. With all its hawthorn trees and scrubby growth, this is a marvellous place for birds.

Beyond another stile the path veers slightly left and uphill under the trees. It then goes to the right and meanders its way to a stile on the left, opposite mature woodland. Cross the stile and turn right into a track, following this down to Speen Bottom by a corner of the wood. Turn right at the Bottom by a bridleway sign and follow the track uphill, soon passing within sight of the attractive flint and brick Kingswood House.

39

As you pass the entrance gate to White House Farm (where the track runs more steeply uphill before curving left) leave the track and join a narrow bridleway on the left. This runs uphill between hedges and connects with a T-junction at the top near bungalows.

Turn right at the T-junction and soon cross a track (the one that you left earlier), then pass to the left of a two-storey house, called Datcha, and enter the field ahead. Follow the field's left-hand edge alongside a hedge to the far corner, where Lacey Green's windmill comes into view. Turn left onto a track, and, passing between houses, join Main Road at Lacey Green. Turning right onto the road, go along to a stile near the road junction. This is next to the bus shelter and a short distance before the Whip public house.

Before crossing that stile this could be a good moment to visit the windmill. Dating from 1650, this smock mill is thought to be the oldest of its type in the country, and has been lovingly restored by the Chiltern Society. It is open from May to September on Sundays and bank holidays, 2.30 pm to 5.30 pm. If you have come on another day you will be compensated by a good view of the mill along the next part of the walk.

From the stile at the bus shelter, go along a field edge to another stile in the field's far left-hand corner. It's more or less straight on now, across a series of fields and stiles, aiming in a somewhat zig-zag fashion (about 60°) towards a high voltage pylon. When you are in the same field as the pylon (passing its left side) you should aim for a stile placed centrally at the far end. As you cross the next field to a stile under trees on the right (90° — straight on) you have the welcome sight of the Pink and Lily, over to your left but distantly.

Once under the trees, go left into a bridleway. This coincides with part of Grim's Dyke, a linear earthwork that makes an appearance (at least in name) in various places throughout the Chilterns. Its purpose and origins are unknown, but it may have served as a boundary in Bronze Age times.

The bridleway soon places you beside Lily Bank Farm, where a left turn followed by ⅓ mile of quiet lane is all that separates you from the Pink and Lily.

Hyde Heath
The Plough

This small, nicely refurbished pub overlooks the comparatively quiet Hyde Heath Road, and across this to Hyde Heath Common. It is a comfortable, friendly place.

The menu starts with conventional pub fare, ploughman's lunches, sandwiches, chicken and mushroom pie, steak and kidney pie, pizza, ham or sausage with fried egg. The home-made category (as opposed to home-cooked, which could have a different meaning!) includes chilli con carne, chicken curry and coronation chicken. Fish meals are of plaice, lemon sole or scampi. The pub specialises in the classic balti dish, made with lamb, chicken or vegetables and 'blended with exotic spices and authentic sauces'. To cool the palate, this could be accompanied by Tetley, Courage Directors or ABC real ales, or by Addlestones draught cider. Alternatively, you could drink Carlsberg Export or Castlemaine lagers. Wine is sold by the glass or bottle. Meals are served every day from 12.30 pm to 2.30 pm and 7.30 pm to 10 pm, except Monday evening (cook's night

off!), and Sunday evenings in winter. The same menu applies throughout. Drinking hours are from 12 noon to 3 pm and 5.30 pm to 11 pm on Monday to Saturday, and 12 noon to 3 pm and 7 pm to 10.30 pm Sunday. The landlord is unswerving in his welcome to families, so much so that you can hardly resist bringing your children here!
Telephone: 01494 783163.

How to get there: Hyde Heath is signposted from the B485, midway between Chesham and Great Missenden (1 mile), and from the A413, between Amersham and Great Missenden.

Parking: In the pub's car park or in Brays Lane near the village hall.

Length of the walk: 3 miles. Maps: OS Explorer 2 Chiltern Hills North or Landranger 165 Aylesbury and Leighton Buzzard area (inn GR 931003).

A walk through fine meadows and woodland, and with a close pass of the magnificent Hawthorn Farm. The route touches the B485 and returns, appropriately, from Halfway House Farm. Back at Hyde Heath Common, you can watch summertime cricket on the green, while any children with you will surely enjoy the play area.

The Walk
On leaving the pub, turn right and soon left into a wide, metalled drive, labelled 'footpath and bridleway', just before the primary school (not opposite Brays Lane). The drive becomes a gravel track and bears right beyond the houses, where there are fields on the right and trees on the left. When you are about 100 yards beyond Lane Gate cottage, go forward through a gap (the branch on the right here is on our return route) and keep straight on alongside a lovely meadow, with a hedge on your left. Ignore a stile on the left quite soon and continue forward into the next meadow, along what is now a concreted farm drive.

Hawthorn Farm (the house) comes into view on the left as you approach a stile at a T-junction. Turn right at the T-junction

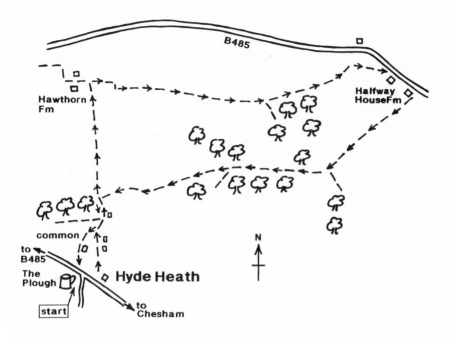

and walk along another concrete drive, going right on it, then left to return to the previous direction. With the house directly behind, follow the drive into the next meadow — where the concrete gives way to flint — and make your exit through a gap at the far end. As the drive (now a track) becomes privatised at this point and enters a wood on the right, you should keep straight on along a field edge, with the wood on your immediate right. A magnificent view opens up as you make your way along the field edge. With the quiet all around you may not realise that the B485 runs along the dip of the next valley, not very far away. Chesham is more apparent, directly ahead.

The wood giving way to a hedge is the signal to keep your wits about you. Don't go charging-on all the way to the bottom of the hill, but look for a stile in the hedge on the right. This is more than three-quarters of the way along the field edge (measured from that gap at the top) and, once encountered, gives a view of Halfway House Farm down on the B485. Once over the stile cross a field downhill to a gate just left of a bungalow (100° — half-right, with respect to your previous

43

Hawthorn Farm.

direction). Turn right in the road there, and, ignoring the first farm gate on the right, right again into the track immediately beyond Halfway House Farm.

What starts as a hard track soon evolves into a grassy path between hedges and takes you straight and true along a dip in the hillside. When after ⅓ mile the path divides at a fork, ignore the left-hand branch (which passes through a gap and heads up to a wood on the left) and continue forward, soon going right with the path and entering a wood higher up. Keep straight on and uphill through the wood (280°), ignoring a branch on the left at the start and shortly entering a meadow.

Keep to the left-hand edge of the meadow and re-enter the wood from the far corner. Ignoring all branches in the track (and noting a field through the trees on the right), leave the wood by continuing forward between hedges. At the end of this stretch, turn left and retrace the first part of the walk — following power lines and passing Lane Gate cottage. For a little variety, you could turn right into a track opposite Troy Cottage and return to Hyde Heath Common by way of The Old Chapel (note the date 1869) and beautiful Autumn Cottage.

44

10 Stokenchurch
The Fleur de Lis

With the M40 taking away much of the A40's traffic, Stokenchurch enjoys relative peace and quiet, especially around the attractive precincts of the parish church. The Fleur de Lis is set well back from the A40, overlooking a wide green.

The food menu offers anything from soup and sandwiches right through to 12 oz porterhouse steaks, including reduced portions for children (at reduced prices). Examples of bar meals are the chef's pie of the day, cottage pie, lasagne and a comprehensive 'all day breakfast'. A choice of vegetarian meals is available, also salads, ploughman's lunches, and filled jacket potatoes. The 'famous hot filled baguettes' come in eight permutations and are freshly made to order. In rounding off the meal, few can resist the tempting desserts when there are such items as 'Fleur de Lis Exotic Banana Boats' and 'Fruits of the Forest Crumble'. Bar meals are available every day from 12 noon to 2.30 pm and 7 pm to 10.30 pm (10 pm on Sunday).

The real ales are Boddingtons, Brakspear and Marston's

Pedigree and the draught cider is the ubiquitous Strongbow. The extensive wine list may be thought inappropriate to a Chiltern ramble — unless I'm mistaken! Drinking hours are 11 am to 2.30 pm and 5.30 pm to 11 pm on Monday to Friday and 'all day' (11 am to 11 pm) on Saturday. Sunday times are 12 noon to 3 pm and 7 pm to 10.30 pm. Dogs may only be taken into the garden.
Telephone: 01494 482269.

How to get there: Stokenchurch is on the A40 west of High Wycombe (7 miles) or can be reached from junction 5 of the M40 (½ mile).

Parking: In front of the pub or in the side roads nearby.

Length of the walk: 2 ¾ miles. Maps: OS Explorer 3 Chiltern Hills South or Landranger 165 Aylesbury and Leighton Buzzard area (inn GR 760962).

This walk explores a magnificent valley lying south-west of Bledlow Ridge, where there are views as fine as any in the Chilterns. It skirts the edge of Stockfield Wood, where there is a good chance of seeing the rare red kite.

The Walk
From the Fleur de Lis cross the A40 to Church Road and follow this round to the oval-shaped green. From the left side of the green a short path leads to the church of St Peter and St Paul. You may not gain entry to the church but you can take delight in the exteriors — in the shingled tower and in the lime-shaded churchyard path. Continue to the far end of the green beyond the Royal Oak pub and turn left into Park Lane. The lane takes you to the right of a small cottage estate and is there signposted as a footpath. Passing a pond on the right and Mallards Court on the left, keep forward along the lane as it goes in and out of a wood to its junction with a metalled drive (do not be unduly concerned about the 'Private' notice beyond Mallards Court, this is a public right of way).
This is a good moment to raise your sights — in the hope of seeing the red kite. A bird of prey that was for many years largely confined to mid-Wales, the red kite is being seen in increasing

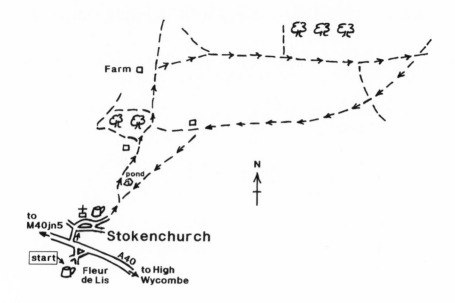

numbers throughout Britain, including this part of the Chilterns. In flight it can be identified by its deeply-forked tail.

Branch left onto the metalled drive (labelled 'Hallbottom Farm') and go down this for 80 yards only, to a stile on the right where the drive curves left. Then cross a meadow, downhill and under electricity wires, to another stile (10°). Passing to the right of the farm and its pond, turn right onto a track (which runs down from the farm) and walk the field edge for the entire length of the right-hand hedge. When the hedge terminates, continue forward along the dip of a wide valley, with Hallbottom Farm in view behind.

Ignore a private track leaving the dip from the left after ¼ mile (it heads up to a wood) and another on the right after a further ¼ mile. Now step thoughtfully! After passing under electricity wires, continue forward about 100 yards to a three-way metal signpost on the left (there are farm buildings in view half-left). Make a sharp hairpin right turn from this point, across the field in the direction of the signpost finger (230° — almost doubling back), aiming for a gap in the hedges near the summit. Steps cut into the bank at the far end of this field path will place you on a track — the private one you ignored earlier. Cross the

Church of St Peter and St Paul.

track to another flight of steps and continue forward, but now along the left edge of a field, with a hedge on the left.

Although the path continues in similar fashion along the next field edge, you may find it easier to use the track running parallel on the left. Whether you join the track here or from the next unobstructed hedge gap, you will in due course arrive at an isolated bungalow. Now hold it there! Your next move is to cross the field on the left, but if you find the prospect too daunting you could stay on the track and turn left at the next junction, making your way back to Stokenchurch on what should be familiar ground. If crossing the field, take your cue from the waymark post just prior to the bungalow and aim for the waymarked electricity pole in the dip in the field (220°, half-left).

Passing to the left of the trees, you will find a stile tucked away 40 yards beyond that pole. This will lead you forward and slightly uphill across a meadow to a pair of stiles, and forward again to another stile and a wide track. Turning left into this track, you will soon find yourself back in Stokenchurch.

⑪ Downley
Le de Spencers Arms

Separated from the vast conurbation of High Wycombe by little more than the cricket green and woodland of Downley Common, the Le de Spencers Arms enjoys a quiet situation along an unsurfaced drive. The building once housed a bakery, as evidenced by the baker's oven discovered in the cellar by the previous incumbent. Inside, the pub is distinctly Victorian — assuming the old valve radio sets pass unnoticed!

The menu includes good, wholesome, home-made dishes, including steak and kidney pie, cottage pie, lasagne, scampi, plaice and cod. Avid meat eaters can indulge in sirloin or fillet steak, while those happy with something less substantial may prefer the salads or sandwiches. These bar meals are served every day from 12 noon to 2.30 pm (2 pm on Sunday) and 6.30 pm to 9 pm, with the exception of Sunday evening. The real ales are Fuller's London Pride, ESB and Chiswick Bitter, while the draught cider is Strongbow. Red and white medium or dry wines are sold by the glass or bottle. The opening times are 11 am to 2.30 pm and 5.30 pm to 11 pm on Monday to Friday, 11 am to 11 pm on Saturday, and 12 noon to 3 pm and 7 pm to 10.30 pm on Sunday. Children are welcome in what I have christened the Snug Room, or in the garden. Well-behaved dogs are allowed, both inside and out. The pub's dog, Tigger, won't mind — he's usually too busy entertaining customers' children!

Telephone: 01494 535317.

How to get there: The pub is along Old Links Road, an unsurfaced drive north of Downley Common and High Wycombe. It is not easy to find! A straightforward approach is from the A4128 Hughenden Road at High Wycombe, by joining Coates Lane along the southern border of Hughenden Park and passing Manor Farm. Once at Downley (near the Bricklayer's Arms) turn right into a 'no through road' and circulate clockwise around the cricket green. At the end of this road turn left into Old Links Road. The pub is straight on — on the right.

Bus 301/302 runs to Downley from High Wycombe bus station. This is a short walk from the railway station where trains run from London (Marylebone). Both services are half-hourly from Monday to Saturday.

Parking: In the pub's car park or in the layby opposite the pub.

Length of the walk: 2¾ miles. Maps: OS Explorer 3 Chiltern Hills South or Landranger 165 Aylesbury and Leighton Buzzard area (inn GR 849958).

The principal attraction along this walk is the National Trust's Hughenden Manor, home of Victorian prime minister Benjamin Disraeli. This is set in the magnificent Hughenden valley, along with Hughenden church, Church House and the Hughenden Stream.

The Walk
Turn left as you leave the pub and go along the rough drive alongside the houses. Where a metalled road comes in from the right and terminates, keep forward with the houses. When the rough drive turns sharp left near a lamp post (not before), go straight on downhill across the common (150° — *not* half-right

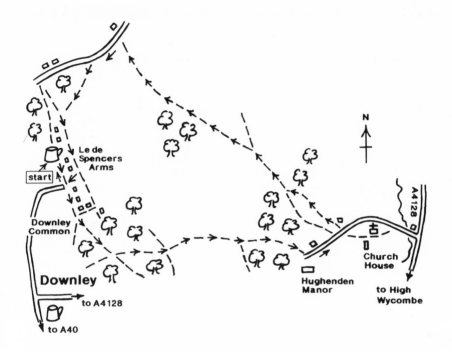

in the direction of distant houses). Entering the wood ahead along a very wide path, soon follow a ditch downhill to a National Trust sign at a seven-way junction of paths. Turn left here onto the only downhill path (90°) and, with a ditch still on your left, stay on this woodland path until it emerges into the open along a dip in the fields. The chimneys of Hughenden Manor can be seen above the trees ahead.

The path re-enters the wood (you should ignore a half-right branch here) and meanders its way uphill, along with the blue arrows, and eventually over a National Trust crossing-path. As a metalled drive, it passes between low flint walls and alongside the entrance gates to Hughenden Manor, with the stableyard (and toilets) opposite. The National Trust shop is nearby. There is also an orchard of unusual apple varieties (doubling as a picnic site) and a reconstructed Victorian greenhouse.

Together with 169 acres of land, the Manor was conveyed to the National Trust in 1947, 100 years after its acquisition by Benjamin Disraeli, who became 'Britain's most flamboyant prime minister'. Disraeli lived at Hughenden until his death in 1881. The house is open on Wednesday to Sunday afternoons from April until October inclusive, and weekend afternoons in March.

Continuing in the same direction, go downhill and over a cattle grid, ignoring a drive coming in from the left just before the grid. For a very pleasant break in the walk you could go downhill across the grass to the church, Church House and the Hughenden Stream. On Sundays and bank holidays from Easter until mid-October (and some Saturdays in July and August) excellent teas can be obtained at Church House. A very worthwhile diversion!

Go through a pedestrian gate a few yards downhill from the cattle grid. This places you on a short concreted path and to the left of a bungalow. A magnificent view of the Hughenden valley is briefly enjoyed while you are taken steeply uphill under the trees. You should ignore crossings and branches and keep straight on up until you arrive at a gate in a field corner. Keep straight on again by following the short field edge to a stile, then turn right through a gate (leaving the wood behind) along a level path between hedges. The right-hand hedge was planted by the National Trust, following their purchase of Naphill Farm in 1989. In their attempt to return the farm to its original field pattern the Trust has very commendably reinstated other hedges in the area.

Now don't go all the way along the path but cross a stile on the left after 200 yards — opposite a National Trust kissing gate. Then cross a large field (310° — half-left with respect to the previous direction), aiming for the left side of a gap between woodland and a clump of trees. On arrival at the gap (at a dip in the field) go forward with the wood edge, ignoring paths leading into the wood. A sequence of stiles and field edges will then take you straight on to a road opposite Oakswood House.

Turn left in the road and go down to a path on the left at the bottom of the hill. Follow this path parallel to, and about 25 yards from, the field edge on the left. Look for a stile on the left after about ¼ mile, and once over this walk alongside a bungalow to a rough drive. Go forward in the drive for 200 yards, branching right opposite Robin's Sheds. A right turn at the end of this short branch will place you back at the pub.

Amersham
The Queen's Head

12

Standing beside the one-time main road to Amersham, the Queen's Head now enjoys the seclusion of a quiet cul-de-sac, while the modern road passes out of sight to the north. Overlooked by fields and woodland, it shares this rural setting with a terrace of attractive cottages.

The menu card is devoted entirely to home-made pizzas, with no less than 12 varieties on offer — in two sizes and as 'regular' or deep pan. The blackboard menu changes from day to day and provides a dozen or so choices, from soup, ploughman's lunches and omelettes to sweet and sour pork, bean and vegetable bake and, in winter, casseroles and game stews. Meals are cooked to order and are available from 12 noon to 2.15 pm and 7 pm to 10 pm daily, but not on Sunday evening. There is a full menu throughout, except on Monday evening when it is limited to pizzas. Children will feel very welcome here. There is a family room complete with high chairs and toys where youngsters can play in safety. They can choose from their own menu or share adult meals, and they can make full use of the swings, Wendy house and so on in the garden — that's if there's time left after chatting to the 20 or so cockatiels, the guinea pig, the rabbit or Desmond the white duck! It is also possible, by prior arrangement, to enjoy a ride around the lanes in the pub's own horse-drawn carriage.

The real ales are Adnams, Rebellion ESB and a guest beer, while the draught lagers are Skol, Labatt's and Carlsberg Export. There is Old English draught cider, as well as wines by the glass and a good selection of malt whiskies. You can enjoy all this, and more, on Monday to Saturday from 11 am to 3 pm and 5.30 pm (6 pm on Saturday) to 11 pm, and from 12 noon to 3 pm and 7 pm to 10.30 pm on Sunday. Dogs on leads can be taken inside, but not in the garden, please.

Telephone: 01494 725240.

How to get there: The pub is situated in a cul-de-sac just off the A404 High Wycombe road, 1¼ miles from Amersham Old Town. Approach along Whielden Lane from the Old Town or from the A413 Amersham bypass. The pub sign stands beside the A404, so you can't miss it!

Parking: The pub does not have its own car park but there is usually plenty of space along the cul-de-sac nearby.

Length of the walk: 2 miles. Maps: OS Explorer 3 Chiltern Hills South or Landranger 165 Aylesbury and Leighton Buzzard area (inn GR 941958).

This short walk approaches the peaceful village of Coleshill along a gently ascending route through woodland and across fields. In Coleshill there is an opportunity to relax by the attactive village pond, admire the many varied cottages and to contemplate the superb windmill.

The Walk
Turn left on leaving the Queen's Head and left again into the path between the garden of end-of-terrace cottage, no 4, and a row of garages. Cross a stile immediately and follow the fenced path as it passes behind gardens and runs uphill to a wood — ignoring two stiles leading into the adjacent field. On entering

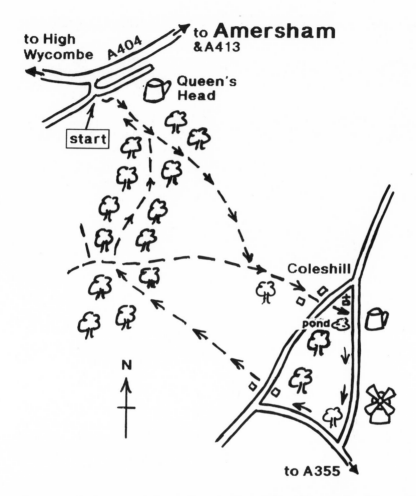

to High Wycombe   A404

to **Amersham** &A413

Queen's Head

start

Coleshill

pond

N

to A355

the wood, ignore a branch on the right after only 20 yards (that's our return path) and keep straight on uphill, following the waymark arrows (130°). After crossing three stiles in a sequence, you will emerge from the wood and enter a field. Go forward 80 yards to a stile on the right near an indent in the field edge (some walkers have arrived at the same point by using a path just inside the trees on the right — perhaps to avoid wet grass!). Having crossed that stile and turned left (straight on if you took the other route) soon cross another stile and go forward into the open.

The pond at Coleshill.

Continue straight on, uphill between fields, with a fence on the left and meeting a waymarked field gate at the top. Turn left through the gate and walk straight on along a drive (grassy at the start) interrupted by a series of gates and stiles, finally alongside gardens to the road opposite Coleshill church. Cross to a path running alongside the churchyard, or walk through the churchyard itself. As described on a handboard in the church, the building was 'started in the mid-1860s to designs by Street, a distinguished exponent of the neo-Gothic. It has beautiful proportions and unpretentious detail . . . and has been praised by Sir John Betjeman.' So it is certainly worth a little of your time — as is the well-placed seat in the churchyard!

That short path (or the churchyard path) places you opposite the Red Lion pub. Turn right here and, passing the village pond, stay with the road when it becomes Windmill Hill. The windmill is still here — behind the houses and looking quite magnificent. Go downhill to a road junction and turn right. Passing Thornbury Cottage, continue downhill to another road junction and turn right into Barracks Hill. Climb the hill to a path just beyond Stock Grove, the first cottage on the left. This path runs alongside the cottage, then through a gap and into a field corner.

Keep straight on, with a hedge on your right at the start, and launch yourself across this very large field. Aim for the right-hand end of a wood at the top of the hill (310°) and, once there, enter this very fine beech wood through a gap. With a field in view to the right, keep straight on again, over a crossing track (which runs into a field on the right) and eventually to a stile and into younger woodland. A narrow, meandering path will then take you to another stile and under more beech trees. After a field comes into view on the left and a path joins forces from the right, go over a stile and downhill between fences. A clockwise circuit of the cottage terrace will then deliver you back to the Queen's Head.

⑬ Chorleywood
The Sportsman Hotel

With its woodland and open space, its ponds, cricket green and attractive cottages, Chorleywood Common is understandably popular with visitors and local residents. And on a windy day it's an excellent place to fly a kite! The lofty Sportsman Hotel is little more than a stone's throw from the common and commands a prominent position overlooking the railway station and the village. It has a delightful family room/conservatory and a garden with a variety of play equipment — wooden horses, climbing frames, swings and a Wendy house. The family room is linked to the upstairs Garden Bar and both rooms are on the same level as the car park. They can also be accessed from the railway station via an outside flight of steps. Overnight accommodation is also available.

The blackboard menu presents a good choice of meals, which is varied from day to day. Typical examples are chicken Kiev, giant mixed grill, Yorkshire pudding with braised steak, grilled gammon steak and deep fried cod. 'Steaks Galore' come in three sizes and are included as one of the special offers. Sweets include strawberries and cream, death by chocolate, spotted dick and apple pie. Meals are served every day from 12 noon to 2.30 pm and 7 pm to 10 pm, but not on Sunday evening. If simple bar snacks (ploughman's lunches and so on) are not available at the time of your visit, you could obtain these along the walk at the Black Horse. Children are welcome there also.

The real ales at the Sportsman are normally Bass and Worthington and the draught cider is Blackthorn Dry. Also on draught are lagers Tennent's Extra, Pilsner and Carling Black Label. Wine (including non-alcoholic wine) is sold by the glass. The Garden Bar is open from 11 am to 11 pm on Monday to Saturday, and 12 noon to 3 pm and 7 pm to 10.30 pm on Sunday. Dogs are normally only allowed in the garden.

Telephone: 01923 285155.

How to get there: The Sportsman stands directly opposite Chorleywood's railway station, where there is a frequent service from the City on the Metropolitan Line and from Marylebone on the Chiltern Line (infrequent on Sunday on the Chiltern Line). Chorleywood (and its station) is signposted from the A404 Rickmansworth to Amersham road, ¾ mile west of junction 18 of the M25.

Parking: In the Sportsman's own car park. Alternatively, you can leave your car in the public parking area on the common. This is opposite the Memorial Hall, a very short distance into the walk.

Length of the walk: 2 miles. Maps: OS Landranger 166 Luton, Hertford and surrounding area or 176 West London area (inn GR 025962).

An easy walk exploring five of Chorleywood's ponds and three of its pubs. It circles the common and, for the most part, keeps clear of the trees. Carefully maintained by the Hertfordshire Countryside Management Service, the ponds are rich havens of aquatic life and a delight to the casual observer.

The Walk

From the Sportsman's car park walk uphill on the drive to the road at the top by the Memorial Hall. Cross to the small public car park on the common (where you may have left your car) and make your exit through a gap on the opposite side. From here strike across the grass towards a dip in the common near a small clump of trees (50°). This point is to the right of a group of buildings, one of which advertises 'Darvell's Joinery'. As you pass to the right of the clump of trees you will find Darvell's Pond nestling within it. What you may not immediately notice is a potential extension to the pond in the form of an earth bund. This was raised in 1994 as part of a scheme to alleviate flooding in Chorleywood after periods of heavy rain.

As you leave the pond and continue forward, it would be best to avoid the horse track and walk closer to the wood on the right, without entering it. You will find yourself coming nearer to the road (on your left) as you approach the next pond. There is a seat here, and another pond a short distance away, by the road junction. You could explore the other pond by following the roadside path in the direction of the road junction.

From the seat and the first of these two ponds (the one furthest from the road junction) you should now move away from the road and join the horse track where it enters the wood on the right. Leave the horse track after 70 yards by turning right into the first clearing, then walk the wide grassy swathe straight on (160°) over two more clearings to a third — where you will find Slady Pond. This is a convenient point for a diversion — left along the clearing to Christ church, the cricket green and (sometimes) the ice-cream van. But please remember which clearing you used, there is more than one!

Back at Slady Pond (with the pond on your right) continue in the same direction as previously and soon turn left under trees bordering a golf course fairway (with the fairway on the right). After passing a golf course green and a seat, dedicated to Merfyn Williams, walk anticlockwise around the nearest adjacent tee — just another green to the uninitiated — and join a narrow path under trees, (120° from the seat). After 30 yards along this path turn right into the horse track and soon arrive at Vicarage Pond. Stay with the track as it curves right and leaves the wood, and as a road comes into view. The rust-coloured rooftops

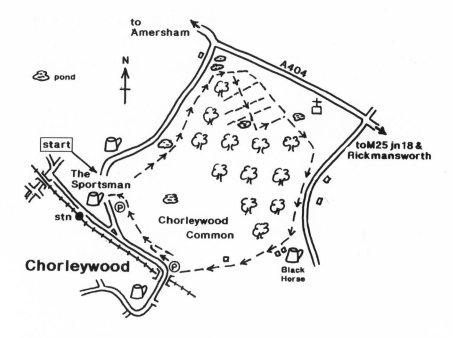

beyond the road are those of Appletree Farm, once the home of Sir Henry Wood, well-known conductor and founder of the Promenade Concerts.

You are now free to move away from the track and walk along the adjacent grass, while aiming for the cottages ahead and uphill. If the Black Horse is your next preferred port of call, you should aim more to the left and downhill, nearer the road. Pass the right-hand side of the uppermost cottage, no 7, by obliquely crossing a flinty track to the summit of the open common. Lark Field, the area of grassland well over to your left, is valued and maintained for its chalk-loving wild flowers.

By keeping close to the trees on the right (240°) and descending the hill, you will pass a pair of cottages (Cherry Tree Dell) along a well-used path, finally arriving at a small car park near the railway bridge. A short diversion to the Old Shepherd is now possible by crossing the bridge. While you are there you could explore a little more of old Chorleywood by descending the short grassy slope to the right of Shepherd's Cottage. A small community of cottages overlooks the slope and extends in both

Slady Pond.

directions along Chorleywood Bottom. You could return to the railway bridge by going left along the Bottom. This will take you past The Retreat, the oldest house in Chorleywood.

Back over the railway bridge look for a narrow path starting near the road and running uphill under the trees parallel to the road and railway. As you approach a small gravel pit (now part of Chorleywood's flood relief scheme), turn right and join the horse track. Go left along this and soon arrive back at the public car park. Before returning to the Sportsman you could indulge in one further diversion — to the Rose and Crown, now in view to your right.

14 West Wycombe
The Old Plough

Once part of the West Wycombe Estate this fine village survives as a remarkable heritage of architectural styles, some of which date back to the 15th century. The Old Plough is at the heart of it all, and is one of the many buildings owned by the National Trust. The pub functions at two levels, the cosy downstairs bar and the upstairs lounge bar. Once you realise that the pub backs onto the hillside you will understand why the garden is also upstairs!

The food choices are divided between the regular bar menu and the specials board. The former includes soup, sandwiches, toasties, filled jacket potatoes and the 'Old Plough Lunch', a ploughman's look-alike with soup added. There is a variety of salads and a number of main meals — beef, Guinness and orange pie, nut and mushroom pie and goujons of plaice being typical examples. The specials board extends the choice to a further five or six items and also includes a selection of puddings — which you will find hard to resist. Meals are available from 12 noon to 2 pm and 5.30 pm to 10 pm on Monday to Friday, 12 noon to 10 pm on Saturday, and 12 noon to 2.45 pm on Sunday. The full menu applies at all of these times. Food can be obtained on Sunday evening but the choice is limited. Children are unreservedly welcome inside the pub (before 8 pm) and can be accommodated downstairs at the front of the pub or upstairs towards the back. This welcome is, of course, extended to the garden.

Three real ales are on offer at any one time, but the brews vary with such rapidity that you could taste eight varieties in the space of two weeks! Gaymer's Olde English cider is on draught, as well as Lowenbrau and Skol lagers. Drinking hours are 11.30 am to 2.30 pm and 5.30 pm to 11 pm on Monday to Friday, 11.30 am to 11 pm on Saturday, and 12 noon to 3 pm and 7 pm to 10.30 pm on Sunday. Dogs are allowed inside but should be kept on a lead and away from the bar.

Telephone: 01494 446648.

How to get there: The pub is easily found — halfway along West Wycombe's High Street. This is on the A40, 2 miles north-west of High Wycombe.

Parking: The pub does not have its own car park and roadside space can be difficult to find. There is a good free car park at the north-west end of the village, beyond the garden centre. This is in Chorley Road a short distance along the walk.

Length of the walk: 2¾ miles. Maps: OS Explorer 3 Chiltern Hills South or Landranger 165 Aylesbury and Leighton Buzzard area and 175 Reading and Windsor (inn GR 828947).

If you can coax yourselves away from this superb village you stand to enjoy an equally superb walk. After taking a gentle path along the lower slopes of West Wycombe Hill the route descends to Chorley Road and the venerable Chorley Farmhouse. It tackles about 150 yards of steep hillside before revealing a magnificent panorama across West and High Wycombe.

The Walk
On leaving the Old Plough go right along High Street to the three-way road junction. Take the middle branch (Chorley Road) and soon join a footpath on the right as directed by a footpath signpost. The path climbs the grassy slope and soon goes under the trees. (If starting from the car park, cross Chorley Road from the exit, then walk uphill and soon turn left onto the path.) Stay on the path until it forks at the first Y-junction. This is after 250 yards and next to a horse barrier. Take the level left-hand branch here (330°) — and not uphill through the horse barrier. This shady path runs just inside the wood and, after a further 350 yards, leads you to another Y-junction, where you should once again take the level left-hand branch (300°). The other branch continues uphill.

Houses come into view along the road below, before the path narrows and descends the hill between over-arching hedges. On arrival at a three-way road junction near the houses, join the branch signposted to 'Radnage' (Bottom Road) and follow this to Chorley Farmhouse, a fine timber-framed house dating back at least 350 years. Pass to the left of the farmhouse and its garden along a track signposted as a bridleway and soon find yourself climbing the hill. The track gets very steep as it runs just inside a wood, and the steepness lasts for about 150 yards — until the track turns left and passes between fields.

Ignore gaps in the tree-line on the left and walk the level track to a waymarked junction of ways. Now take care! Keep straight

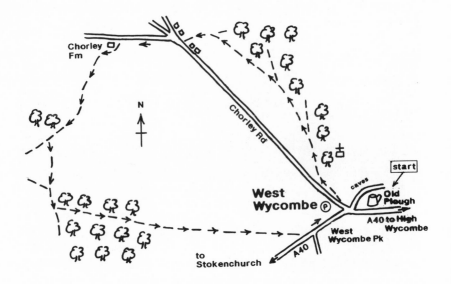

on, but for 40 yards only, to the corner of a wood, where there is a 'No Horses' sign. Climb the bank here and join a waymarked path running straight on through the wood. Taking guidance from the arrows (about 100°), eventually cross two tracks and emerge from the wood at a stile. The stile places you in a field near a corner of the wood and provides a marvellous view across West Wycombe to High Wycombe.

For the final leg of the journey you should now aim for the far extremity of the right-hand hedge (not the wood edge). Alternatively, take your direction from the aerial mast beyond High Wycombe. Keep straight on when the hedge terminates and go downhill across two fields in succession, finally joining the A40 at West Wycombe. As you descend the hill you have one of the best views of the National Trust's West Wycombe House.

Turning left on the A40 you will see the beginnings of the river Wye, which normally starts life in the field on the left and joins the Thames at Bourne End. After noting the Pound at the road junction ahead (where stray animals were kept until claimed), turn right into High Street for the Old Plough or left for the car park.

West Wycombe Park.

Places of interest nearby

Depending on your reserves of energy you could follow up the walk with a visit to *West Wycombe Caves*, the *church* and *mausoleum* on the summit of the nearby hill or *West Wycombe House* with its beautiful grounds and lake. The grounds are open on Sunday and Wednesday from 2 pm to 6 pm in April and May, the house and grounds on Sunday to Thursday from 2 pm to 6 pm between June and August.

Penn
15 The Crown

The popularity of the Crown is due in part to its situation on a busy B road, but also to its attractive setting — opposite the parish church and the lovely cottage terrace in St Pauls Hill. The main bar of the pub is located in a part of the building dating back many centuries, while the Wheelwright's Bar is a reminder of a trade that was followed here in earlier days. Not surprisingly, the coffin-maker that worked here does not have a bar named after him!

The 'Country Carvery' menu offers starters, hot platters, salads, ploughman's lunches and sandwiches. Examples of the hot dishes are steak and kidney pie, fish and chips, gammon steak and chicken Kiev. The specials board lists more interesting choices, with a variety of hot meals, salads, children's favourites and sweets. Meals are normally served from 12 noon to 2 pm and 6 pm to 9 pm daily (7 pm to 9 pm on Sunday), with a slightly reduced choice on the two busy days — Saturday and Sunday. Although there is no family room as such, the carvery/

restaurant is an ideal place for children to eat and drink with their families. If you have a dog with you, the preferred place for him is in the garden.

The real ales are Webster's Yorkshire and Courage Best and Directors, while the draught ciders are Strongbow and Scrumpy Jack. There are French house wines and speciality wines, all by the glass or bottle. Lagers include Foster's, Kronenbourg 1664 and Budweiser. The drinking hours are from 11.30 am to 2.30 pm (note the slightly earlier closing time than is usual) and 6 pm to 11 pm on Monday to Saturday. On Sunday the times are 12 noon to 3 pm and 7 pm to 10.30 pm.

Telephone: 01494 812640.

How to get there: The Crown is easily found. It is on the B474, 2 miles north of Beaconsfield and junction 2 of the M40.

Parking: In the pub's car park or alongside the B474 a short distance east of the pub.

Length of the walk: 2¾ miles. Maps: OS Explorer 3 Chiltern Hills South or Landranger 175 Reading and Windsor (inn GR 917933).

This walk dips in and out of Penn Bottom on its way to the estate land of Penn House. Being surrounded by a perfect balance of woodland and cultivated fields, Penn Bottom is as attractive as its name suggests. A glimpse of Penn House is enjoyed, and more than a glimpse of its fine trees and pastures.

The Walk

You will find a two-way footpath signpost at the upper corner of the pub's car park, under the Crown sign. Go into the field here and follow its right-hand edge, initially parallel with the B474. Soon curve left with the field edge, moving away from the B474 and following instead a narrow sunken lane — which is almost out of sight. You could join the lane if you wish, through a gap on the right, keeping straight on when it meets another lane. Otherwise continue to the far right-hand corner of the field (under an electricity pole) and then follow overhead wires for about 50 yards to a stile on the right. This will place

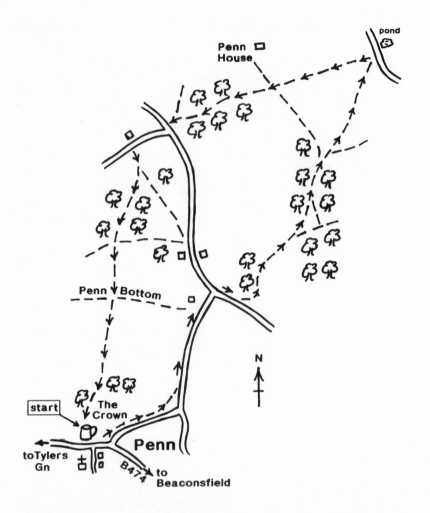

you on that country lane. Turn left and go downhill towards
Penn Bottom.

Before arriving at a T-junction in the Bottom you will notice
a collection of sarsen stones. These large stones are hardy
remnants of an overlying stratum of sandstone and were
excavated following cable-laying and extension work on
Church Knoll, the attractively-gabled house nearby. Turn right
at the T-junction and go along this lane (in single file!) for 75
yards to a signposted track on the left. The track will take you

effectively straight on between a wood-edge and a field (ignore a branch going into the wood at the start). The track soon curves left around the wood — which later gives way to a hedge, and the hedge to a short gap. The gap gives you a brief view of two fields on the left while the track takes you forward into the wood.

When the track divides just inside the wood, take the main branch, the one going straight on (40°). This runs parallel to the wood edge (with a field in view on the left) and soon joins the metalled drive to Penn House. Ignoring a left-branching track very soon, go forward on the tree-shaded drive almost until it turns left. From this point veer very slightly right along a woodland track (50°), keeping straight on at a waymarked dividing of ways after a further 50 yards.

When you eventually arrive at a stile by a quiet road (opposite a pond) you should double back to another stile leading into a pasture, with your back to the road. A path may be evident running across the pasture — if not, take your bearing from the line roughly set by the two stiles in series (260°). A glimpse of Penn House (which is privately owned) is obtained as you cross the pasture, and a stile at the far end leads you onto its drive. After crossing the drive to another stile, cut across the short right-hand end of a field and enter a wood. Go straight on under the trees (260°) and soon downhill, eventually meeting a stile at the right-hand end of a magnificent avenue of lime trees. Complete the descent by joining a road at a T-junction.

Climb Common Wood Lane opposite (straight on) to a stile and signpost on the left, almost opposite Beechwood Cottage. Cross the field here at right angles to the road (160°) and enter the wood on the far side. Once in the wood turn half-right immediately and go uphill for 30 yards to a clearly-marked divide in the path. Take the right-hand branch (straight on, 200°) and continue uphill. When you emerge into the open at the summit of the path continue forward, but now on a wide path across a very large field. Penn is in view ahead, Tylers Green half-right.

Having descended to a dip in the fields (Penn Bottom) go over a track and ascend the opposite slope to a wood at the top. After going right briefly, follow the waymarked path as it meanders uphill through the centre of the wood (200°) and takes you to

Sarsen stone.

a stile. From here you will have sight of the Crown's garden, and very soon the Crown itself.

As a tailpiece to the walk you could circle around Holy Trinity churchyard opposite the Crown (anticlockwise is best!). As you do so, notice the '1736' above the brick chancel (the date of its rebuilding), also the magnificent flint tower with its rare one-handed clock, and the 15th century main entrance door. Inside you will find one of the treasures of the church — a 15th century painting on oak boards above the chancel arch.

Places of interest nearby

If time is on your side you could also explore *Tylers Green*, a ¾ mile drive from the Crown. Children will love the green and the pond. This is a delightful place — and the secondhand bookshop is well worth a visit.

16 Skirmett
The Frog

Keeper's Cottage, The Old Post Office, Isabel Cottage, Ramblers, The Old School — these are just a few of the beautifully maintained cottages that adorn this lovely village in the Hambleden valley. The Frog is equally well cared for, and makes a particularly pretty picture on flowery summer days. If you knew the pub under a different name you may be puzzling over the 'Frog'. Drop the 'S' from Skirmett and all is revealed! Go inside and see the little Muppet hero portrayed everywhere. It's hardly suprising that children love it here.

The lunchtime menu includes cottage pie, filled jacket potatoes, ploughman's lunches, seafood open sandwich (very popular with regulars) and the multi-layer club sandwich. The indelicately named 'Belcher's Beauty', with its kidney beans and garlic, is designed for those who like to make their presence felt. Children can have smaller portions of anything (at smaller prices). They are welcome in the family-cum-games room or in the Lily Pad (along with Kirmett), the pub's 'no smoking' dining room. Food is available from 12 noon to 2 pm and 6.30 pm to 9.30 pm on Monday to Saturday, and 12 noon to 2 pm and 7 pm to 9 pm on Sunday. There is a special supper menu in the evening. En-suite accommodation is also available.

The real ales include 'Frog Hopper' from Belcher's brewery and Old Luxters, brewed locally. The lagers are Foster's and Kronenbourg. Beamish stout is on offer, together with a good selection of wines. The Frog is open for drinking on Monday to Saturday from 11 am to 2.30 pm and 6 pm to 11 pm, and on Sunday from 12 noon to 3 pm and 7 pm to 10.30 pm. Well-behaved dogs are permitted in the bar or games room.

Telephone: 01491 638996.

How to get there: Skirmett is ¾ mile south of Fingest, and Fingest is signposted from the A40 at Piddington, 1 ½ miles west of West Wycombe. It is also signposted from the A4155 at Mill End between Henley and Marlow.

Parking: In the pub's car park or along the roadside 100 yards north of the pub.

Length of the walk: 3 ¾ miles. Maps: OS Explorer 3 Chiltern Hills South or Landranger 175 Reading and Windsor (inn GR 775902).

As the walk makes its gradual ascent of the Hambleden valley, it reveals fine views both east and west. After a brief sojourn along quiet roads at Pheasants it returns to the valley floor. Here lies the Hamble Brook (except in times of drought!) and a series of lovely meadows to escort us back to Skirmett.

The Walk

On leaving the Frog go left along the road to a rough drive on the right beyond The Old Forge. This will take you past the village hall to a stile just left of a bungalow. After crossing the stile go forward a few yards and turn right to pass behind the bungalow. Follow a fence and overhead wires until they part company, then bear right alongside a hedge and stay with it to a stile and a lane (170°). Turn left in the lane and go along this for 25 yards to where it curves left, and join a bridleway on the

74

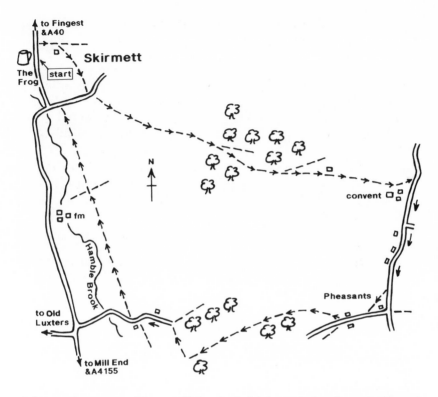

right under trees. You will be led fairly painlessly uphill and provided with lovely views east and west. In less than ½ mile you will arrive at a waymarked Y-junction at the entrance to Hatchet Wood. Take the right-hand branch (straight on) and continue going up. Perhaps the most attractive part of the wood is a clearing which has been replanted after storm damage.

As you leave the clearing you should ignore a branch going off to the left and continue straight on — while a field makes its appearance on the right. After passing a lovely flint and brick house on the left and going forward along its drive, you will find yourself in sight of Parmoor House and its outbuildings. Having noticed the chapel (with its stained glass windows), you will not be surprised to learn that Parmoor is a convent. The house is on the 'List of Buildings of Special Architectural or Historic Interest'. Hopefully, the house is not as sad and

The Old Post Office.

neglected as the grounds. Turn right in the road here and soon pass the entrance to Parmoor, and after that Little Parmoor — which is not exactly little!

Keeping straight on along this road, you will find a footpath sign on the right just beyond a crossing of power lines. Leave the road here and walk up a short drive until it goes left towards a house, then keep forward across the grass to a stile and enter a meadow. Cross the meadow to a stile in the furthest corner (about 210°) and join a road there. Nearby you will find a pond, and The Old Pheasant, the Pheasant pub until the 1940s.

Turn right in the road and go as far as a signpost opposite Beeches Farm — before the road makes its 1 in 5 descent. Cross two stiles here and aim for the opposite corner of the meadow (290°), near the right-hand extremity of a line of trees. From a stile in that corner continue straight on, soon following a timber garden fence and then passing under trees to a field corner. Go along the left-hand edge of this very long field, with a wood on the left, to its far left-hand corner. Turn right here and walk the short field end (parallel to the Hambleden valley) to a stile. The stile is tucked away in the corner and leads to a path running straight on under trees. This soon meets the drive to Bagmoor, where you should turn left.

After passing The Hyde and its tennis court (where the track becomes a metalled road) look for a stile on the right leading into a meadow. Before climbing that stile you could continue the short distance to the Hamble Brook, a lovely stream running down from Skirmett along the Hambleden valley to the Thames at Mill End. After crossing the stile you have a ¾ mile sequence of meadows and intervening stiles to take you back to Skirmett. Keep straight on all the way, parallel with the valley and taking your direction from the windmill on the heights above Turville.

Your arrival at Skirmett will be at a stile that appears to the right of a low flint barn. Turn left on the road here and take the first right for the Frog.

Places of interest nearby

Not far from Skirmett, *Old Luxters Brewery, Winery and Gallery* would make an interesting excursion with which to end the day. It is signposted from the Hambleden road 1 mile south of Skirmett and is open daily until 6 pm (5 pm in winter). Admission is free.

17 Nettlebed
The White Hart Hotel

One of the two remaining hostelries in Nettlebed (there were five in the 1700s), the White Hart stands with other historic buildings beside the busy A4130, the old coach road from Henley to Oxford. Among the hotel's military associations is its use as a billeting house in the Civil War and as an unofficial mess for RAF personnel in World War II. Douglas Bader was a frequent customer and scenes from the film *Reach for the Sky* were made here.

Children are very welcome here and have their own menu — a 'Menu with Children at Hart'. Amongst its delights are 'Sally's sizzling sausages', 'Charlie's chunky chicken nuggets' and 'Penelope's pan fried pizza'! Adults can choose from various snacks, such as ploughman's lunches, omelettes, salads and sandwiches or from the main menu or specials board, which together feature an extensive range of choices. The pudding list is full of irresistible dishes all made on the premises. These meals are served from 12 noon to 2 pm and 6 pm to 10 pm on

Monday to Saturday, and 12 noon to 3 pm and 7 pm to 9.30 pm on Sunday. Come here in winter and enjoy the warmth of the real log fires; come any day and enjoy afternoon tea (from 2 pm to 6 pm — 3 pm to 7 pm on Sunday). Hotel accommodation is also offered.

The real ales are from Brakspear. Henley Strong Ale is available (for consumption *after* the walk perhaps — if you are not driving), and there is an extensive choice of wines by the glass. The bar is open for drinking for the maximum time allowed, 11 am to 11 pm on Monday to Saturday, 12 noon to 3 pm and 7 pm to 10.30 pm on Sunday. Dogs are permitted inside if well behaved.

Telephone: 01491 641245.

How to get there: Nettlebed is on the A4130, midway between Henley and Wallingford. The White Hart is easily found — along the High Street. Bus 390 from London (Buckingham Palace Road) to Oxford stops at Nettlebed approximately two hourly every day.

Parking: The White Hart has its own car park but you are asked not to leave your car there while on the walk. There is alternative parking space alongside the common a short distance along the walk.

Length of the walk: 3 miles. Maps: OS Explorer 3 Chiltern Hills South or Landranger 175 Reading and Windsor (inn GR 700868).

There's a marvellous feel about this walk — along the tree-shaded drive to Soundess House, across fields by Warburg Nature Reserve, and in the confluence of valleys below Berrick Trench. And there's a fascinating industrial history — symbolised by the preserved pot kiln at the start of the walk and the abandoned clay pits towards the end.

The Walk

From the White Hart go left along the High Street and cross the B481 to the village shelter (not the bus shelter). The magnificent pot kiln nearby is a reminder of the brick, tile and pot industry that existed in Nettlebed from the Middle Ages. A display panel

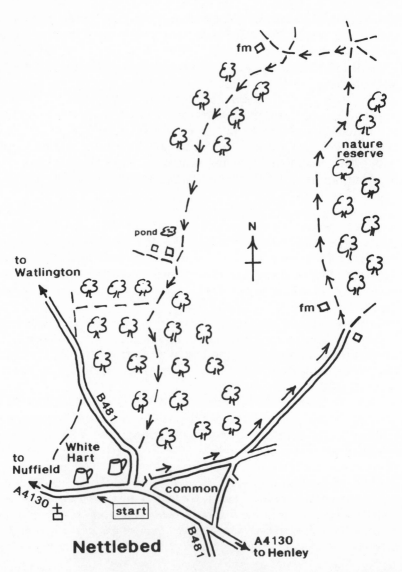

to Watlington

to Nuffield

A4130

White Hart

B481

start

common

B481

A4130 to Henley

pond

fm

nature reserve

fm

N

Nettlebed

at the base of the kiln gives more information, including the fact that this is one of five known kiln sites in the area. Go along the road that runs between the common and the houses (Malt House and others) and follow this to a road junction. Branch left along the road signposted to 'Magpies' (not 'Crocker End') and stay with it when Soundess House is announced. A fine avenue of trees takes over and the road finally terminates at a lodge cottage.

Turn left along a wide track between woodland and a field, and, passing Shepherds Cottage en route, stay with the track until it turns right. Leave the track here and enter the field ahead. When the wood gives way to a hedgerow (more accurately, a 'tree-row') at a dip in the field, climb a pair of stiles on the right and go downhill just under the trees along a field edge. The wood on your right is part of the Warburg Nature Reserve, owned by the the Berks, Bucks and Oxfordshire Naturalists Trust.

A superb view is yours to enjoy as you make your way down to a stile and as you cross the next field half-left (360°) to where the valleys meet. A stile at the bottom will place you on a junction of ways where you should turn left. With the field now on your left, go along the track for 250 yards to a stile on the left under electricity wires. This is just before a wood on the left and in sight of farm buildings. Follow the wood edge uphill a short distance to a farm track and go over this to a stile. Entering the wood here, follow the path as it curves a little to the right and takes up its position along the summit of a ridge (230° when on the straight), with a field in view about 50 yards to the left.

Having kept more or less straight on along the ridge, you will eventually leave the wood from a stile. You will then be over-looking a dip in the field running forward towards a distant house. You should cross that dip obliquely (straight on), aiming for a line of beech trees on the left side of the field (180°). Once there, walk forward under the trees to a stile, and then pass to the left of a pond and its guardian statue. Keeping to the left-hand edge of a large well-manicured lawn, soon go along a wide path under trees and meet a rough drive that leads to that and another house.

Turn left in the drive and stay with it through the wood for about 130 yards only — to where it turns half-right. Great care is now required — although the next stretch through the wood is waymarked with arrows, you may find that the paint has faded! Leave the drive here by going straight on along a footpath. Then, after counting 80 man-size paces (65 yards), turn half-left (150°) along with the arrows. When, after a further

Cottages in Nettlebed.

80 paces, you arrive at a distinct crossing-path, go over this and slightly right. Continue straight on at a fork after 30 paces. A few yards prior to a T-junction in the path, turn left and soon find yourself beside a Thames Water manhole cover. Turning left from the cover (150°), advance the last few yards to the blunt end of a rough drive just outside the wood.

In spite of all this concentration you may still have noticed the numerous clay pits throughout the wood. These are vestiges of the intensive brick and tile industry that existed in Nettlebed's past (remember the pot kiln?). Follow the drive down to the B481 and turn left. Passing the Sun (another excellent pub), turn right into the High Street and return to the White Hart.

The wrought iron gates in view as you turn into the High Street lead to the house and grounds of the Sue Ryder Home, Joyce Grove. You are invited to quietly walk through the grounds; a lovely way to end your day — and an unforgettable experience.

Bovingdon Green
The Royal Oak

18

Bovingdon Green, a triangular-shaped open space surrounded by houses old and new, is 'just around the corner' from the Royal Oak. The pub itself is attractively sited adjacent to the village pond.

From the regular food menu you can have ploughman's lunches, salads, including the 'Royal Oak Special', sandwiches (toasted or untoasted and with a choice of 'off the bone' ham), filled jacket potatoes and desserts. The 'House Specialities' is a list of about ten dishes, including steak and kidney pie, Cajun chicken or fish, vegetarian lasagne and cauliflower cheese. The choice is expanded by the specials board, which is regularly re-written. Children are very welcome inside in the dining areas away from the bar, also in the large garden to the rear. Outside barbecues are fired-up at weekends when the weather is well behaved. Food is available from 12 noon to 2 pm and 7 pm to 10.30 pm on Tuesday to Sunday, except Sunday evening. Note that Monday is rest day for Cook (the landlord!). You are, however, welcome to eat your own sandwiches in the garden on that day — if you are buying drinks.

The real ales are Wethered Bitter, Brakspear Bitter and Wadworth 6X. On good summer evenings a mobile bar is brought into action in the garden. Drinking hours are from 11 am to 3 pm and 5.30 pm to 11 pm on Monday to Saturday, and 12 noon to 3 pm and 7 pm to 10.30 pm on Sunday.

Telephone: 01628 483875.

How to get there: Bovingdon Green is 1 mile from Marlow. It is signposted near the Red Lion pub where the A4155 doubles as Marlow's West Street.

Parking: In the pub's car park.

Length of the walk: 2½ miles. Maps: OS Explorer 3 Chiltern Hills South or Landranger 175 Reading and Windsor (inn GR 835870).

Commencing from the attractive green, the walk soon enjoys a view of the Thames valley, including a little of the Thames itself. It penetrates the popular wooded levels of Marlow Common and passes Monks Corner, an interesting house once occupied by the novelist and playwright Jerome K. Jerome.

The Walk
Turn left as you leave the pub and, passing the pond, turn first left into the road signposted 'Bovingdon Green'. Aim for the far right-hand corner of the green and join a rough drive there, going forward on it for a short distance to a signposted path on the left — beyond the end of a hedge. This narrow path runs between a hedge and a field and soon curves right to follow the field edge. In due course the path passes through the hedge to the other side and continues in the previous direction. As you walk on the left side of the hedge, a view of the Thames valley is revealed, with a glint of reflected light from the river.

The path evolves into a wide track under the trees and descends to a clearing. Go over a stile on the right near the bottom of the hill and enter the wood. Now take great care! Follow the path as it climbs gradually through the wood (about

84

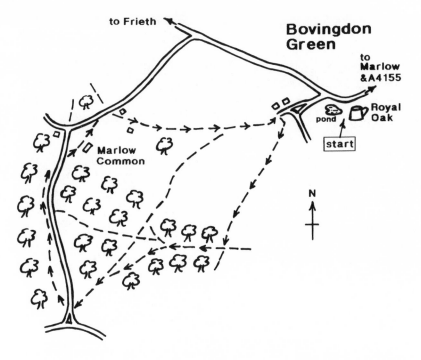

280°) and look for the first branch on the left. This branch is 250 yards from the previous stile (where you entered the wood) and is clearly waymarked. It will take you uphill (along with the waymark arrows) and close to a field on the left (260°). Keeping that field in sight and walking parallel to a ditch and dyke for part of the way, eventually join a road (at a fork) on the tree-clad Marlow Common.

Cross the road and continue forward for 30 yards to a ditch and dyke under the trees (not to be confused with the earth bunds at the roadside). Turn right there and follow the waymarked path alongside the dyke, more or less parallel with the road (360°). At a crossing-path after ¼ mile a notice announces the Woodland Trust. This society is dedicated to the conservation and maintenance of trees and woods including ancient woodland.

You can either continue forward under the trees or on the road alongside. Whatever your choice, another 250 yards will place you by a fenced enclosure to the left of the road. Go ahead

85

Monks Corner, Marlow Common.

on the road to a signposted path on the right opposite a gate in the enclosure. This runs half-right with respect to the road and soon places you in front of Jerome Cottage and Monks Corner. Built in the early 1900s, Monks Corner was for a time the home of Jerome K. Jerome, well known for his *Three Men in a Boat*. Notice the intriguing linked chimneys and the beautiful 'Della Robbia' friezes. It is interesting to identify the activities depicted by each frieze — without trespassing of course!

Go forward along the drive here and turn right onto the road at the end. Leave the road after only 50 yards and join a drive on the right, just before a pole-mounted transformer. When the drive runs into the garden of Heather Croft continue forward, but now along a grassy path between a meadow and a garden hedge. After crossing a stile you should go straight on across the centre of a meadow to another stile (90°), then across the corner of the next meadow to a stile along its right-hand edge. Once over that stile, turn left onto a path between a hedge and a fence and soon join a drive going forward to Bovingdon Green. Walk to the far end of the green and turn right for the Royal Oak.

Stoke Row
The Cherry Tree

19

While Stoke Row owes its popularity to the Maharajah's Well, the Cherry Tree owes its name to the abundance of cherry trees in the district. This is one of a dying breed of no-nonsense pubs, where sociability is the order of the day. Though modest, the pub has a certain claim to fame — it was here in 1964 that HRH Prince Philip dined following attendance at the centenary celebrations for the Maharajah's Well. A signed sample of water drawn from the well by the Prince still stands on a mantelpiece near the bar.

Simple but adequate lunchtime snacks are available on Tuesday to Saturday from 12 noon to 2 pm, and on Sunday from 12 noon to 1.30 pm. There are filled rolls, sandwiches, ploughman's lunches, salads and home-made quiche. If you prefer something hot you can choose from steak and kidney pie, pasties, mushroom or spicy chicken slice. Jacket potatoes come with various 'dips' rather than pre-filled. In the evenings (Tuesday to Saturday from 6 pm to 10 pm) the choice is limited to one or two items only. If you arrive at other times you might persuade the licensee or his wife to make you a filled roll. With its small 'away from the bar' lounge, its games room and its garden play area, the Cherry Tree is a good place for children.

The pub has an excellent reputation for the quality of its ales. These are Brakspear Mild, Bitter, Special and OBJ (Oh Be Joyful — otherwise described as Rocket Fuel!). Strongbow cider, Heineken and Stella lagers and Guinness are on draught. Drinking hours are the traditional 11 am to 3 pm and 6 pm to 11 pm from Monday to Saturday, and 12 noon to 3 pm and 7 pm to 10.30 pm on Sunday. You may take your well-behaved dog into the garden, but not inside the pub, please.

Telephone: 01491 680430.

How to get there: Stoke Row is signposted from the A4130 by Nuffield Golf Course, 1½ miles west of Nettlebed, and from the B481 at Highmoor Cross, 1½ miles south of Nettlebed. The pub is in the main street.

Parking: In the pub's car park or in Newlands Lane between the chapel and the green.

Length of the walk: 2¾ miles. Maps: OS Explorer 3 Chiltern Hills South or Landranger 175 Reading and Windsor (inn GR 684840).

A fine walk across gently rolling Oxfordshire countryside — through woods, across fields and along quiet country lanes. There is a superb view of Whitcalls, a red brick mansion, at the half-way point.

The Walk
On leaving the pub turn left in the main street and take the second left into Newlands Lane between the chapel and the green. Stay on the lane as it turns right then left. When it again turns left keep forward along a waymarked path running downhill into a wood (30°). When the path divides at a fork after 100 yards take the left-hand branch (10°) and continue downhill through the wood. After a further 150 yards go over a crossing and through a pedestrian gate, ignoring all branches until you find yourself on a road under trees at the bottom.

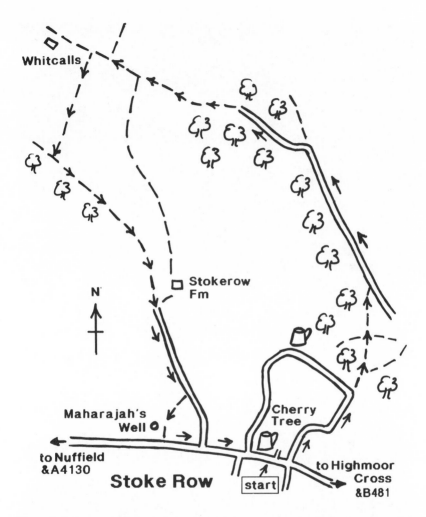

Whitcalls

Stokerow
Fm

N

Maharajah's
Well

Cherry
Tree

to Nuffield
&A4130

Stoke Row

start

to Highmoor
Cross
&B481

Turn left here and, passing a tennis court on the left, stay on the road when it eventually turns left, ignoring a track going forward from this point.

The road soon turns right and climbs the hill, losing its tarmac beyond Oakingham End. It loses the trees also, and becomes a hedge-lined path between fields. Ignore the first stile on the left and look carefully for the second. This is about ¼ mile from where you left the trees and about 200 yards before the red brick Whitcalls Farm. You may find it hard to believe that this

Maharajah's Well.

very grand Georgian-style house was built as recently as the 1980s — and on the site of a pig farm!

Going left over the stile and passing a cattle trough immediately, cross a field alongside a wire fence and at right angles to the previous path (200°). A sequence of two more stiles will take you to a T-junction with another path under trees, where you should turn left.

After ¾ mile the path passes the entrance drives to Stokerow Farm and evolves into a tarmac lane. Continuing forward on the lane for less than ¼ mile, look for a waymarked path on the right just beyond The Pond House. This path runs alongside a hedge and soon places you on Stoke Row's main street, where you cannot fail to notice the Maharajah's Well, set in an attractive public garden and complete with elephant!

Opened in 1864, the well measures 368 ft in depth and provided the village with no less than 600 gallons of water per day. It came about through a friendly association between Edward Anderdon Reade of Ipsden and the Maharajah of Benares. For a complete rendering of the story you should read the information board near the well.

A left turn in the road will take you past a public open space. This was originally planted with 101 cherry trees, the crop being sold to help maintain the well. A corner of the open space is now planted with a play area. So if you are not accompanied by children on this walk, you will soon be back at the Cherry Tree.

⓴ **Gallowstree Common**
The Reformation

Reformation and Gallowstree — two names demanding an explanation! The Reformation was 'reformed' from a bakery in the mid-1800s and Gallowstree was a place of execution for offenders brought here from Reading Gaol. More of the latter as we proceed on the walk.

As for the Reformation, rarely can a pub be such an attraction to children. In addition to an adventure play area (scramble nets, slides, log bridge and so on), it has a fascinating collection of animals — pygmy goats, rabbits, chipmunks and ducks, and aviaries housing about ten species of tropical birds. If, with all this, children can be persuaded to come inside, they may be taken into the snug room or the pool/function room. Here they can choose from the 'Just for Children' menu, which includes items they will find hard to resist — 'Fishysaurus' and 'Turkeysaurus' for example!

With the Reformation's Declaration in hand (the menu!) adults cannot escape similar entertainment. There is a variety of dishes including 'Lawyer's Lament' (home-made lasagne), 'Plaintiff's Plea' (chicken breast marinated in lemon juice) and 'Bow Street Runners' (beef and vegetable pie). Filled jacket potatoes and ploughman's lunches also have their legal connotations. And if you are 'Too Late to Reform' you can indulge in an amazing choice of 'puds'. All this can be enjoyed without distraction, during Sunday lunchtimes in winter, by placing younger children in the crèche (for a small charge). Meal times are 12 noon to 2 pm and 6.30 pm to 9.30 pm daily (7 pm to 9 pm on Sunday evening). The full menu applies throughout these times. The real ales are Brakspear Mild, Special and Ordinary. Strongbow cider and Heineken and Stella lagers are on draught. In winter the pub's own-recipe mulled wine is designed to warm those parts that cold beer cannot reach. The drinking hours are 11 am to 2.30 pm and 6 pm to 11 pm on Monday to Saturday, and 12 noon to 3 pm and 7 pm to 10.30 pm on Sunday. Good dogs on leads are allowed inside the pub. Please note that the caged birds and animals may become alarmed by lively dogs in the garden.

Telephone: 01734 723126.

How to get there: Gallowstree Common is signposted from the A4074 at Cane End (by The Fox public house) 5 miles north of Reading. This approach will take you direct to the Reformation (¾ mile).

Parking: In the pub's car park. Alternatively, you can leave your car in Hazelmoor Lane, which branches from the main street midway between the pub and the petrol station.

Length of the walk: 3 miles. Maps: OS Explorer 3 Chiltern Hills South or 175 Reading and Windsor (inn GR 690802).

This straightforward walk explores the woods, clearings and peaceful lanes north of the village. The woods are largely beech — with huge specimens creating a unique atmosphere — and the clearings a storehouse of new growth. Wyfold Farm is met at the halfway point. Here the old barns and stables have kept their beauty and are a delight to the passer-by.

The Walk

From the pub go left along the main street and left again into the road opposite Hazelmoor Lane. You will see the old village well on the right almost immediately. This enjoys the status of a 'Listed Building of Special Architectural or Historic Interest' and the virtue of being more than 100 years old and about 200 ft deep. A true centenarian! Stay with the road until it turns left, then go through a barrier on the right to a junction of paths. Take the half-left branch, passing behind the garden of Elsinore and keep to the main path as it enters a beech wood. A cricket green will come into view about 20 yards to the left, followed by a field. When, after ⅓ mile, you arrive at a point adjacent to the corner of this very long field, turn left into what may not at first be a very clear path (260°). You should find a waymark arrow pointing that way, and when you are on the correct course the field will again be on your left and a low bank on your right.

Follow what soon becomes a good, clear path all the way to a lane by the attractive flint and brick Kate's Cottage. Less attractive is the history hereabouts, for nearby stood the gallows of Gallowstree, a row of beech trees where offenders were hung for such petty acts as sheep stealing, a punishment last meted out in 1826. Turning right on this quiet lane, pursue it for ⅓ mile until you see a bridleway sign on each side — where the field on the left gives way to woodland. Leave the road here and join the right-hand bridleway. This runs at right angles to the lane, between established woodland on the right and regenerating woodland on the left. Notice that the trees are now of many varieties — lime, beech, hazel, oak, cherry and more. Ignore a branching path on the right after 75 yards and keep straight on, eventually to another quiet lane.

Turn right onto the lane and in due course come in sight of the barns of Wyfold Farm, now converted to residential use. With their rust-coloured bricks and tiles and delicate brick patterning they make a superb picture. While passing between the houses and the farm, notice the very fine stable block on the right, and, after the lane curves right, the earth bank along the boundary of Wyfold Grange. The latter is the rampart of an Iron Age fort, within which the Grange was built.

After the lane curves right, and just beyond the drive to

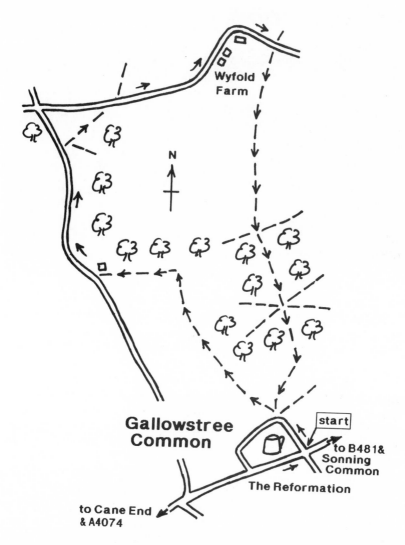

Wyfold Grange, turn right into a path signposted 'Gallowstree Common 1'. This directs you across a field to a dip where this and other fields intersect (190°). From the dip go forward and uphill along the right-hand side of a tree-row. The path soon leaves the field edge and continues uphill inside the tree-row, finally entering Wyfold Wood from a stile. Passing a pond at the

Old Well at Gallowstree Common.

start, keep straight on through the wood (about 160°), following the waymark arrows and ignoring all branches.

Stay with the path when it crosses a clearing and places you back amongst the bungalows where the walk started. The quickest way back to the pub is the reverse of the outward journey — a left turn in the road here, followed by a right turn in the main street. For a little variety, however, you could turn right in the road then left in the main street.